MW01071080

Sue Lawrence is an Edinburgh-based food writer and author who has written many books on cooking and baking, including *Scots Cooking* (2000), *Book of Baking* (2004), *A Cook's Tour of Scotland* (2006), *The Scottish Soup Bible* (2017) and *A Taste of Scotland's Islands* (2019). She has also written six historical novels, including *Lady's Rock* (2024).

New Scottish Baking

SUE LAWRENCE

BIRLINN

Opposite: Chocolate brownies (and Raspberry brownies), p. 87

First published in 2024 by
Birlinn Limited
West Newington House
10 Newington Road
Edinburgh
EH9 1QS

www.birlinn.co.uk

Text copyright © Sue Lawrence 2024

All photography © Katie Pryde, 2024
(*www.katieprydephotography.co.uk*),
except pages 27, 50, 101, 119, 131, 139, 177, 191,
and 214, which are courtesy of the author.

The right of Sue Lawrence to be identified as the author
of this work has been asserted by her in accordance with
the Copyright, Designs and Patents Act 1988.

All rights reserved. No part of this publication may be
reproduced, stored or transmitted in any form without
the express written permission of the publisher.

ISBN: 978 1 78027 868 1

British Library Cataloguing-in-Publication Data
A catalogue record for this book is available from the British Library

Designed by Mark Blackadder

Papers used by Birlinn are from well-managed
forests and other responsible sources

Printed and bound by PNB Print, Latvia

For Matilda, Harris, Oliver, Iona and Ailsa, with love

Contents

Opposite: Linzertorte (aka Posh jam tart), p. 198

Introduction

I have lived and breathed baking ever since I can remember. And in Scotland this does not mean fancy iced buns, cupcakes laden with thickly piped icing or garishly decorated gateaux. No, for us in Scotland it is the homely smells of freshly baked treacle scones, sultana cake and, of course, shortbread – the aromas that greeted me as I walked through the door after school – that sum up Scottish baking. Nothing fancy, but oh so delicious.

The cake tins in my home – and everyone else's, when I was a child – were filled with baked goods such as gingerbread and fruit loaf for visitors popping in. It was all just part of growing up. And when my children were young, they too would come home to baking smells and to cookie jars filled to the gunnels. Nowadays it's my grandchildren who get to open the cake tins.

The many church fêtes, school fairs and gala days of my youth featured home-baking stalls. And just like those still allowed under the stringent health-and-safety legislation today, the baking was and is always the first to go. There would be fruit scones, cherry and coconut slice, home-baked biscuits, Scotch pancakes and, of course, tablet wrapped in greaseproof paper, all laid out in serried rows, ready for the onslaught. The minute the doors opened, there was a rush, an unseemly surge towards the baking stall, which was known to sell out in minutes. Heaven help anyone trying to reach the tombola, if they were in the path of the baking fans intent on their purchase.

Scottish baking has evolved over the years. The old recipes have been adjusted to add less sugar and the unhealthier fats are often removed, though the traditional favourites still remain as popular as ever. Since I wrote my first baking book in 1996, however, so much has changed on the baking scene. When *The Great British Bake Off* began to air in 2010, viewers loved the escapism of watching a tent full of eager bakers trying to create the perfect scone or brownie. All these years later, it's now a worldwide phenomenon, with spin-offs in many countries, including France, whose *Le Meilleur Pâtissier* is a huge hit – and not only in France. I, too, am addicted. The millions of people who regularly watch *Bake Off* are a new breed of baker – people who enjoy creating delicious cakes and traybakes, inspired by those they see weekly on television.

There are also the lockdown bakers. During those strange and lonely months of being forced to stay at home during the first phase of the covid-19 pandemic, as well as yoga and family quizzes on Zoom, there were many who turned their hands for the first time to baking. Banana loaf and sourdough bread were two of the most popular recipes researched online; everyone had so much more spare time. Many of these new bakers, who found such satisfaction and pleasure in creating delicious bakes when the whole world was shut down, continue baking with joy.

Opposite: Flapjacks, p. 257

There are now many wonderful new cafés where there is not just a tired piece of days-old Victoria sponge on offer. Everyone has upped their baking game in the past couple of decades, and even in the most remote café there will be a freshly baked cheese scone or a delicious piece of buttery shortbread on offer with your flat white.

Since baking has become the new hip pastime, there are many other baked goods that we Scots now love to both bake and devour. It is not just scones and Dundee cake that you find in cafés and that people are trying out at home; from pains aux raisins and focaccia to rocky road and green tea cookies, there are exciting new delights to enjoy with your coffee or tea. There is always something – traditional or modern – to satisfy our insatiable sweet tooth.

This book is about new Scottish baking. Yes, it contains many traditional recipes, but I have also included many contemporary ones to tempt your tastebuds. As well as being comforting and delicious, homebaking is surely the most generous form of cookery. Think about it: When did you last bake a cake just for yourself? It's all about sharing. Baking is a slice of pie or a piece of shortbread made with love, then offered with joy.

A Note on Ingredients

Here are some common baking ingredients and recommendations.

I started off, as a child, baking with margarine instead of butter (apart from shortbread, of course!) but now would never use it. I also used Scotbloc instead of proper chocolate: anathema these days! So these are guidelines to the ingredients I prefer to use myself, but none are prescriptive. Use what is available and what you can afford.

FLOUR

If you have a choice or are able to buy flours from smaller or artisan mills, then these are worth trying:
- Barony Mill, Orkney (beremeal)
- Scotland The Bread
- Mungoswells Malt & Milling
- Hodmedod's flours
- Shipton Mill
- Doves Farm
- Matthews Cotswold Flour
- Bosse Dahlgren's Heritage Grains Project at Ardross Farm (with kind permission from the Pollock family)

Plain versus self-raising flour

Most bakers in this country have a stock of both plain and self-raising flours in the cupboard. But if you find you are out of self-raising, then just add baking powder to plain flour: for 200g plain flour, you need 2 teaspoons of baking powder.

Strong white flour

Strong white flour has a higher protein content (12–14 per cent) than regular plain flour (8–10 per cent), which is why the latter is best for pastries and cakes, and strong flour is essential for breads and buns. The higher protein content creates more rise and enables the final product to hold its shape.

Gluten-free flour

Commercial gluten-free flours provide excellent results. They are usually a mixture of rice, maize, buckwheat, potato and tapioca flours. If I am making shortbread for someone who is gluten-intolerant, I use gluten-free flour and rice flour – the texture is nicely crunchy and short. Most baking powders are gluten-free, too, but do check the label. The two brands I use include rice flour and maize flour in their ingredients, both of which are gluten-free.

EGGS

I use large eggs, unless otherwise stated, and always free-range.

SUGAR

I try to use unrefined sugar, as the flavour is much better. I recommend opting for light and dark muscovado sugars instead of 'soft light' or 'soft dark' brown sugars. Though we Scots are renowned for our sweet tooth – and mine is pretty pronounced – I'm not sure I could revert to my childhood days of stealing sugar lumps from the table when out for tea, then sucking them through teeth that were surely about to need fillings at the dentist! Or dipping raw rhubarb from the garden into bowls of white sugar, as my sister and I did every year in the early summer. But I do love sugar in baking. So, since I seldom use it, why not use the best available, which, in my opinion, is unrefined.

FATS

Always butter, never margarine, is my rule; and only unsalted butter, unless I'm making shortbread, when I like slightly salted. Although margarine used to be considered the healthier option, since it is lower in saturated fats, some soft margarines and spreads are made with hydrogenated fats, which convert some of the unsaturated fats into trans fats. The latter, when used in food processing, have been linked with some degenerative illnesses. As a general rule, if a spread contains hydrogenated fats, it will probably contain trans fats.

It is advocated that margarine makes the lightest cakes and I am not going to deny this; this is because margarines are whipped up during the hydrogenation and blending process. But provided you beat the butter thoroughly, until pale – often with the sugar – before adding eggs, flour and so on, you too will have a light cake.

And as for flavour, baking with good butter or refined margarine? No competition. The true flavour of butter wins hands down over margarine every time. Olive oil can also be used in certain recipes and, as with butter, use the best possible – extra virgin – but do try to use an oil that is not overtly peppery.

When a recipe asks for softened butter, by the way, it is butter that you can poke your forefinger into and it leaves an indentation. If you want to soften hard butter, you can use the microwave, but check every couple of turns, as it changes from rock solid to molten liquid in a flash whenever your back is turned.

YEAST

Fresh yeast is a pleasure to use, but since it can be difficult to find, I have given all recipes with fast-action (sometimes called easy-blend) dried yeast. If you can find fresh yeast, buy it (it freezes well) and use 15g for every 7g sachet of fast-action dried yeast. With fresh yeast, you need to blend it first with a little tepid water and a pinch of sugar, then add to the flour and other ingredients after 10–15 minutes, or when it has begun to froth.

SYRUP/TREACLE

In Scotland, 'syrup' means golden syrup and 'treacle' means black treacle. I realise this seems as if I am stating the obvious, but in the south of England treacle is often interchangeable with syrup; indeed, treacle tart is famously made with golden syrup!

Both are gloriously sticky and gloopy, and this can pose problems when measuring them. The easiest ways to obtain the correct amount is to either first dip the spoon into boiling water, or very lightly oil the spoon first. You can also lightly flour your scales before weighing the treacle or syrup.

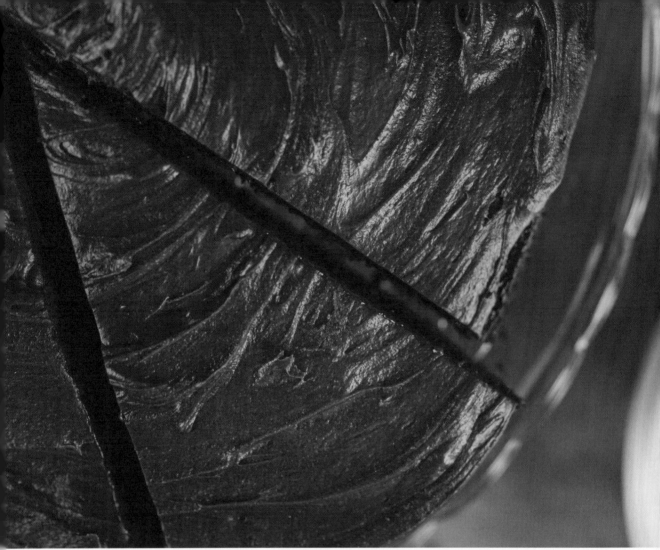

Above: Chocolate Coca-Cola cake, p. 147

CHOCOLATE

'Best quality' chocolate is specified in all the recipes here. The difference to the taste is incomparable. Best quality means that dark chocolate should have over 50% cocoa solids, but I think over 60% is better. Unless otherwise specified, aim for 60–70% cocoa solids. Dark chocolate with cocoa solids over 75% is almost too bitter for baking and you may need to up the sugar content. Milk chocolate ought to have over 30% cocoa solids, and for white chocolate ensure it is the very best quality you can afford, as there are some overly sweet sickly bars out there.

To melt chocolate, either place it in a heatproof bowl over a pan of gently simmering water or microwave it, set to a medium/high heat until almost melted. With both methods, break it up into small pieces first.

A couple of other notes on the book:

FREEZING

I freeze everything. Well, not every single thing, but much of my baking – unless it's wolfed down all in one sitting. Once cool, just cling film or pop in a freezer bag and freeze. I can't give you specific 'Best Before' dates, as every bake varies, but as a general rule things that should be eaten fresh, such as scones, freeze well but should not be frozen for as long as, say, a fruit cake.

You can also freeze iced cakes: just 'open freeze' – which means popping them in a freezer shelf once iced, without any covering, then once the icing is solid, overwrap in cling film. I would not leave iced cakes too long in the freezer – perhaps a couple of weeks tops.

Pastry also freezes well. Any leftover bits and pieces I wrap in cling film and freeze, though do ensure you mark clearly whether it is sweet or savoury pastry. Accidents can happen . . .

A handy tip is if you have rolled your pastry into your tart tin and you don't have an hour or so to wait as it chills in the fridge, you can pop it in the freezer instead, for only about 20 minutes, then take it from there.

OVEN TEMPERATURES

I've given temperatures for conventional (non-fan-assisted) ovens, so please adjust accordingly.

TEASPOONS/TABLESPOONS

All teaspoons and tablespoons are level, unless otherwise specified.

1
Bread

Introduction

I was not brought up with home-made bread – no one I knew had freshly baked bread emerging from their ovens when they came home from school. Rather, it was scones, buns, shortbread or a slice of simple sultana cake from the tin.

I spent every summer and one whole year in France during my years studying at university and I never encountered home-made bread. That would have been unthinkable. Why bother, when you only had to pop along to the local *boulangerie* twice a day for the most delicious baguette?

I lived in northern Finland for a year after that and though I did not encounter home-made bread, for the first time I did see a lot of fresh yeast. Wonderfully squidgy and beery smelling, the yeast was sold in even the tiniest supermarkets, primarily to make pulla (cardamom buns) and enriched sweet bread dough, for wonderful Finnish fruit and berry cheesecakes and pies.

For three years in the early 1980s I lived in northern Germany, and it was then that I began to come across home-made bread more frequently. Sometimes it was flavoured with rye; almost always it was delicious.

Back in the UK, home-made bread was often heavy and dense, as most of us really didn't know what we were doing. But gradually home-made loaves became less worthy and thankfully lighter, more palatable, and indeed usually better than the supermarket equivalents.

Many years later came the pandemic lockdown, and with it sourdough. There had been a surge in artisan bakeries over the previous decade or so, which meant until then we didn't even have to bake our own sourdough bread, but with lockdown, things changed and loaves appeared all over social media!

I recommend trying a home-made loaf, if only to see how delicious it can be. The following breads are some of my favourites.

BREAD TIPS AND VARIATIONS

- In order to achieve the perfect temperature for 'tepid' or 'hand-hot' liquid, mix one-third boiling liquid to two-thirds cold. Basically, it should feel pleasantly and comfortably warm, never hot.
- Unbleached flour gives far more character to a loaf.
- Ensure you have enough salt in your dough, otherwise it will be tasteless.
- Fast-action or easy-blend dried yeasts are my preferred options, as they are always to hand. If you use fresh yeast, use 15g dissolved in some tepid liquid, with half a teaspoon of sugar, and leave to stand for 10–15 minutes. This mixture is added along with the tepid liquid in the recipe.

Previous page: Classic loaf, p. 21

- You can replace some of the tepid water with tepid milk; this gives your bread less of a chewy texture and more of a soft crumb.
- The easiest way to incorporate liquids into dry ingredients is to make a 'well' in the centre of the dry ingredients and gradually pour in the liquids with one hand, while 'drawing in' the flour with a spoon held in the other.
- The wetter the dough, the better the bread, so add enough to make a softish but not too sticky dough (if you add too much liquid, it will be impossible to knead).
- Kneading by hand is my preferred method – it is also the best stress reliever! You can knead in a food mixer using a dough hook. Or try the no-knead recipe (p. 22).
- To knead by hand, stretch the dough away from you with the heel of your hand, then turn the dough and repeat the movement. Ten minutes is usually enough for the texture to change and become smoother and more elastic.
- When allowing bread to rise, we normally talk about a first and second rising. To check if you have kneaded the dough enough in the first stage, gently press it using your fingertip: if it springs back, it is ready. To check if it has risen enough during the second rising, again gently press in a fingertip – this time it should not spring back. Rather, it will leave an indentation, which means the gluten has stretched as much as possible and it's ready to bake.
- The ideal temperature for bread dough to rise is 20–25 °C (which is the temperature of most airing cupboards), but you can leave it for an hour or so longer just at room temperature. Never leave it somewhere hot, such as on top of a radiator, and ensure your bowl is tightly covered, so it is draught-free. I place bowls of dough on a wire rack above my heated kitchen floor.
- Regular dough will take 1–2 hours to rise (my house is cold, so I allow 2) but enriched dough takes an hour or so longer. Slowly risen dough has a better taste and texture.
- Leaving a dough to rise overnight in the fridge is perfect if you have guests the next day – you achieve the homely bread-baking aromas but you have done the hard work of measuring and kneading the day before! This method also ensures a truly flavoursome loaf after a slow-rising. Simply cover the bowl of kneaded dough and place it in the fridge for at least 12 hours. Next day remove to room temperature (the dough will be harder than usual), knock back and shape as usual, but give the second rising longer. I usually leave it for at least an hour.
- To 'knock down' or 'knock back' means to punch a risen dough with your fist to deflate air bubbles: this takes place after the first rising.
- Loaves can be glazed: brush with beaten egg, or beaten egg yolk or milk, before baking – or with olive oil, milk or melted butter immediately after baking. You can also simply dust with flour, fine oatmeal or fine polenta prior to baking.
- To test whether bread is cooked, remove and turn upside down with oven gloves, then tap the loaf underneath: if it is ready, it will sound hollow, like a drum.

Classic loaf

This basic recipe can be modified, depending on taste. Try adding in a handful of sunflower or pumpkin seeds – or substituting a quarter of the white flour with a rye or granary variety. Though, I have to admit, I like it just as it is: simple and straightforward, delicious with butter and jam or honey, or with butter and cheese or ham. Butter, you will notice, is the key, always.

Mix the flour and yeast in a bowl with the salt.

Make a well in the centre and slowly pour in enough water (about 450ml) to make a softish dough.

Using floured hands, bring the dough together and turn it out onto a floured board. Regularly sprinkling (lightly) with flour – I use a flour shaker – knead for 10 minutes until smooth: it should be soft and shiny-looking, but no longer sticky.

Place in an oiled bowl and cover with cling film, then leave somewhere vaguely warm for 1½ – 2 hours (I place mine on a wire rack over my heated kitchen floor: it takes 2 hours to increase its volume to almost double).

Lightly oil two baking sheets or two 500g loaf tins.

Punch down the dough with your fist and divide into two, then shape into two loaves, tucking ends underneath. Place on the baking sheets and cover loosely with oiled cling film, or place the dough, tucks underneath, into the two loaf tins.

Preheat the oven to 220°C.

Leave the dough to rise again, somewhere vaguely warm, for about 45 minutes – or until it does not spring back when gently pressed with your finger.

Using a sharp knife dipped into a flour bag (to prevent sticking), slash the top lightly to form slits, then dust with flour and bake in the preheated oven for about 25 minutes or until the base sounds hollow when tapped.

Remove to a wire rack and cool completely before slicing.

Makes 2 loaves

•

700g strong white flour

7g sachet fast-action dried yeast

2 tsp salt

450ml tepid water

No-knead loaf

Makes 1 loaf

•

500g strong white flour

1 tsp fast-action dried yeast

1½ tsp salt

350ml water

This astonishingly easy recipe gives such a good result – and with so little effort. Just mix, leave to rise, shape into the tin, leave to prove, then bake. It is utterly delicious.

It has, perhaps, a slightly closer crumb than the classic loaf, but it is by no means dense.

The essential ingredient here is time: once mixed, since you have not kneaded it to develop the gluten, you must allow the loaf a long, slow rise – at least 12 hours.

There are a couple of differences to note if this is the first time you are trying no-knead bread. The water, instead of being tepid, should be at room temperature. And when you leave the dough for the first rise, do not place it somewhere warm; it needs to be room temperature. Only for the second rise/prove, should it go somewhere vaguely warm.

Combine the dry ingredients in a large bowl and add 350ml of water at room temperature (mine is always freezing cold from the cold tap, so I add a few splashes of boiling water). Mix well with a spoon, then combine to a dough: at this stage it will be very bitty and scrappy. Cover with cling film and leave at room temperature for 12 – 18 hours.

Lightly butter a 1kg loaf tin.

The dough will have risen and so, using floured hands, scoop it out and place it on a floured board. Roll it up into a short log-like shape, then place in the loaf tin. Loosely cover and leave somewhere vaguely warm (I place mine on a wire rack over my heated kitchen floor) for a couple of hours until well risen.

Preheat the oven to 220°C.

Slash the top of the loaf three times with a sharp knife dipped in flour (to prevent sticking). Place the bread in the oven for about 35 – 40 minutes until baked through, covering the top loosely with foil after 20 minutes. Test by upending the loaf and tapping the base: it should sound hollow.

Remove to a wire rack and cool completely before slicing.

Sourdough loaf

To make sourdough there is an investment of both time and energy. You are in it for the long ride. But while patience is required, the minute you see bubbles begin to form in the starter, the excitement builds.

I have baked for so many years, but I must confess that I am relatively new to the mystique of sourdough. And while I don't bake sourdough regularly, I do find that this recipe works well for me (it is based on one my Shetland friend Isabel Johnson uses). It took me three attempts, mind you, to achieve loaves that not only tasted good but looked pretty good, too.

Sometimes it is difficult to shape the bread into a perfect loaf or ball; most professional bakers use a banneton or proving basket. You can recreate this by placing the shaped dough into a bowl lined with a heavily floured cloth. But as long as you don't mind too much how perfect your loaf looks, you can use a well-oiled bowl thickly sprinkled with flour, as per my instructions. The main thing is the taste – the long, true, old-fashioned flavour – and the chewy texture, with a good crisp crust.

———

Several days before you want to make the bread, begin preparing the starter. Place 50g of strong white flour in a large Kilner jar (or other deep receptacle – I like glass, as you can watch the action inside) and add 75ml of tepid water. Stir, seal and leave for 24 hours at room temperature. The next day, add the same amount of flour and 50ml of tepid water. Leave for another day, then repeat this (you may need slightly less tepid water – you want just enough to make a thick consistency; it should not be too runny). Stir the mixture and seal every time.

By around the third day you should see some large bubbles forming. The next day, the bubbles will be smaller but there will be more of them and the smell will have become nicely yeasty. You can usually use the starter from day 5 or 6. It should be fairly thick and gloopy, rather like a thick pancake batter.

When you are ready to make the bread, weigh out 175g of the starter and mix with approximately 225 – 250ml of tepid water (enough to make it combine to a thick dough). Because the dough will be rather sticky, I like to use my mixer and dough hook. Place the flour and salt in the bowl of the mixer, add the starter mixed with water, and begin on a low speed till combined, increasing to medium, for 8 – 10 minutes or until the dough is smooth and elastic. You can also knead by hand on a floured board. Most sourdough bread recipes recommend using a 'stretching and folding' action, rather than kneading, but you can use whichever method you are comfortable with. To stretch and fold, you simply pull up half the dough with one hand to stretch it, then fold it back in, turn it around 90 degrees, then repeat.

Makes 2 small loaves

•

175g sourdough starter
(see recipe for instructions
and ingredients)

225 – 250ml tepid water,
plus extra for the starter

500g strong white flour

2 tsp salt

Place the (now smooth) dough in a well-oiled bowl, cover and leave somewhere vaguely warm for 2 hours (I place the bowl on top of a cooling rack over my heated kitchen floor).

Tip onto a lightly floured board and stretch and fold for a few turns before returning to the oiled bowl, covering and leaving somewhere warmish for another hour.

Divide the dough into two and shape each into a ball, creating two loaf-shapes, tucking the ends underneath. Have a second oiled bowl ready, then sprinkle each with a good layer of flour (this replicates the floured cloth favoured by most sourdough bakers). Now place each ball of dough, seam-side up, in a bowl, cover with cling film and leave somewhere warmish for 2 – 2½ hours or until they have risen.

Preheat the oven to 220°C and place a baking sheet on the oven shelf. Once it has reached the correct temperature, place a (deeper) baking tin in the bottom of the oven with some ice cubes, to create steam, which helps form a good, even crust.

Remove the baking sheet and shake over some flour from a flour shaker. Tip out both balls of dough and sit them on the baking sheet so the tucks are now underneath, slash the top with a sharp knife dipped in flour (to prevent sticking) and place in the hot oven above the tin of ice.

Bake for about 20 – 25 minutes or until a golden crust has formed and they sound hollow when tapped on the base.

Cool on a wire rack before slicing.

Aga loaf

Though I have to rely on my friend Hils, who is a brilliant cook and baker, for any Aga bakes, I realise how wonderfully handy an Aga is. You don't even have to think about Stage One in regular baking, which is Switching On the oven. With an Aga, it is always hot and ready.

You can use a variety of strong flours for this – granary or wholemeal, or a mixture of white and brown.

Mix the flour in a bowl with the yeast and the salt.

Make a well in the centre and very slowly pour in about 550ml of tepid water – just enough to combine into a soft dough.

Using floured hands, tip the dough onto a floured board and knead for about 10 minutes, flouring lightly as you knead.

Place in a lightly oiled bowl and cover with cling film, then leave to rise for about an hour near the warmth of the Aga until the dough has more or less doubled in size.

Punch down the dough, then knead again for a minute or so, then shape into a long oval shape and place on a buttered baking sheet. Cover with oiled cling film and leave again somewhere warm for a further 30 minutes or so until puffed up. Remove the cling film, snip along the top of the loaf and dust with flour.

To bake, place the grid shelf on the floor of the roasting oven and place the baking sheet on top. Bake for 25 – 30 minutes or until golden brown. When tapped underneath, it should sound hollow.

Remove to a wire rack and let it become completely cold before slicing.

Makes 1 loaf

•

700g strong white flour

7g sachet fast-action dried yeast

2 tsp salt

550ml tepid water

Morning rolls (baps)

Makes 9

·

700g strong white flour

2 tsp salt

40g lard or butter, diced

7g sachet fast-action dried yeast

425ml tepid water

semolina flour or fine semolina, to sprinkle

Morning rolls, as they are often called in Scotland – or baps, as you might know them – are perfect for breakfast, as they are soft, floury and unchallenging as the first food of the day. It is only later on that you feel ready for a well-fired or extremely crusty roll, which can also be hard work on the jaws! In Aberdeenshire, baps are usually called 'softies', if they have no flour on them, and 'floury baps', if they do. In Glasgow, you might hear them called Mortons rolls, after the baker whose shop was founded in Anniesland in the 1960s.

My parents both remembered from their Dundee childhoods being sent to the baker's for morning rolls before breakfast at weekends; weekdays, it was porridge. Just as we have the vision of every French household sending someone for the morning baguette, so the Scottish family sent a minion (usually the youngest member) for breakfast rolls.

According to F. Marian McNeill, whose *The Scots Kitchen* (1929) is one of the best reference books on old and traditional Scottish recipes, in the sixteenth century baps were sold at nine for twelve pence. And so my recipe is for nine good-sized rolls. They are wonderful split and spread with butter and eaten with bacon, egg, sausage or – my favourite – black pudding and tomato.

When I was at Dundee university, after a late night out we students headed home via Cuthbert's, just off the Hawkhill. Anytime after midnight – and, indeed, all night long – you could get a 'morning' roll warm from the oven and filled with butter – or cheese (another of my favourites). The Dundee speciality was mince. The greasiness of the hot mince roll was perfect to soak up the odd glass of shandy drunk during the evening.

These rolls were not well fired. Rather, they had a pleasingly (but not challenging) crispy crust to them and that divine soft, fluffy dough on the sides where they had been pulled apart from their neighbours. A bit like the edges of a batch loaf.

Memories of these late-night rolls still linger after many decades, and they are recreated here – though seldom partaken of, these days, as a means of staving off a hangover the following day. Now they are a treat for breakfast or lunch, or indeed any time of day. Just maybe not in the wee small hours.

***

Mix the flour and salt in a bowl, rub in the lard or butter, then stir through the yeast.

Make a well in the centre. Gradually pour in about 425ml of tepid water, then using lightly floured hands bring together into a dough.

Turn this out onto a lightly floured board and knead for about 10 minutes or until you can feel it change texture from rough and nubbly to smooth and elastic. You can also knead it in a food mixer using the dough hook for about 5 – 6 minutes.

Place this in a lightly oiled bowl and cover. Leave to rise somewhere vaguely warm for 1½ – 2 hours or until well risen. (I put mine on a wire rack over my heated kitchen floor.)

Line a baking sheet with parchment paper.

Sprinkle some semolina onto a large board. Knock back the dough, to punch out the air, then divide into nine pieces. If you want them to look uniform, weigh each piece – they should be about 125g each. Shape the pieces into rounds, first tucking any joins underneath, so that the top is convex.

Roll lightly under the palm of one hand, your fingers forming a sort of cage with claw-like fingers.

Once they are all shaped, sprinkle again lightly with semolina, then, using a rolling pin, roll each ball out very gently to flatten it just a little.

Place them on the lined baking sheet – three rows of three – ensuring they are all touching so you get the characteristic soft fluffy sides when you pull them apart.

Cover loosely and leave for 45 – 50 minutes in a vaguely warm place until well risen. During this rise, preheat the oven to 240°C.

Once risen, bake for about 15 minutes or until puffed up and golden brown.

Eat warm.

Aberdeen rowies (butteries)

Makes 16

•

600g strong white flour

7g sachet fast-action dried yeast

1 tsp caster sugar

2 tsp salt

350ml (approx.) tepid water

200g butter, softened

sprinkling of sea salt

'I'm making do with a coffee and a rowie, the region's own flattened, salty version of a morning roll, designed to keep for a week on a heaving trawler or something, allegedly.' These words in Ian Banks's brilliant book *Stonemouth* describe Aberdeenshire's national bread beautifully.

And for those assuming the word 'buttery' must involve butter, sorry to disillusion you: it has never been traditional to use butter. It was always 'white fat' or lard, although original Aberdeen fishermen's 'rowies' were made with butcher's dripping or lard. They were designed to last, so they could be eaten on long trips away at sea.

I prefer the flavour of butter, however. And though my recipe uses only butter, you could just as well make them with lard for a truly authentic flavour. They are the perfect accompaniment to soup or salad and taste good with cheese. I don't think they need a thick smear of butter on top, as is the norm in Aberdeenshire; to my taste, they are buttery enough. But for a real treat, head to the Contini Scottish Café and Restaurant beneath the National Gallery in Edinburgh and try the eggs florentine – poached eggs, hollandaise sauce and a scattering of fresh chilli on freshly baked butteries. It is a taste sensation.

Make the bread dough by placing the flour in a bowl. Add the yeast, sugar and salt. Once well mixed, add enough of the tepid water to combine to a dough. Turn onto a board and knead for 7–8 minutes until smooth. Place in large bowl, cover and leave somewhere vaguely warm for a couple of hours until risen.

Punch down and roll out with your palms to form a rectangle.

Cut the butter into three long slices. Add a third at a time, to a third of the bread dough, then fold over and continue with the remaining thirds. It is a folding process, like making puff pastry. Now, using well-floured hands, either knead by pushing and folding and turning the dough until you can see the butter is incorporated, or, if you prefer, 'chop' in the fat by hand, with the blade of a blunt knife, a pastry scraper or the long edge of a palette knife. Once well combined, the dough will be slightly sticky.

Cut into about 16 pieces and place these on a lightly floured (not buttered) large baking sheet. Shape them by pressing the front part of your (floured) hand – fingers only – onto each, so they are flattened and dimpled with fingerprints with one stroke. Sprinkle some sea salt over the top of each, then cover with oiled cling film and leave to prove somewhere warm for another 30 minutes or so.

Preheat the oven to 230°C.

Bake for about 20 minutes until crispy and golden. Remove to a wire rack to cool.

Seaweed soda bread

This recipe is based on one shared with me by my friend Maggie Darling. Hers uses a mixture of dried dulse, shony and kombu seaweeds, but I prefer to use only dulse, as the pure, tangy flavour – and colour – shines through. Dulse is usually brownish-red when fresh, becoming almost purple by the autumn, towards the end of the harvesting season. I use Mara Seaweed's dulse; the dried seaweed is not only excellent but also incredibly handy in its little 10g pouches.

Unlike yeast-raised breads, you must employ a light touch for soda bread – it's more like making scones than bashing out yeasted dough by kneading. The trick with soda bread is to simply pat it gently into shape, never roll, and certainly never knead.

This bread is best eaten on the day it is made, preferably with lashings of butter. It is the most perfect accompaniment to a bowl of hearty soup. It is also delicious thinly sliced and spread with a smear of cream cheese and topped with a good slice of smoked salmon. Next day, it is good toasted.

The recipe uses milk that is soured by lemon juice, instead of buttermilk (but use approximately 325ml of buttermilk, if you prefer), so you need to start this process in advance.

––––––––––

First, stir the lemon juice into the milk and set aside for about 20 minutes or until it looks a little lumpy.

Preheat the oven to 190°C. Lightly oil a baking sheet.

Mix together the flours, oatmeal, bicarbonate of soda, baking powder and salt. Stir in the dulse and make a well in the middle.

Add the egg and most of the liquid (you may not need it all), then draw in the flour to combine to a rough dough, which should be soft but not sticky. Bring it together with floured hands and place on a floured board. Shape it into a long oval shape, about 4cm deep. Slash with a sharp knife dipped in flour (to prevent sticking) four or five times across the top and place on the baking sheet.

Bake for about 30 minutes, until well risen and nicely browned, then remove from the oven. Place the baking sheet on a wire rack and flip the loaf over. Leave it to sit on the hot baking sheet for at least half an hour (it will continue to cook), then remove to the wire rack to cool completely before slicing

Makes 1 loaf

•

juice of 1 small or ½ a medium lemon (about 25ml)

300ml milk

250g plain flour

200g seeded bread flour (or wholemeal flour with seeds added)

50g medium oatmeal

1 tsp bicarbonate of soda

3 tsp baking powder

1 tsp salt

2 rounded tbsp dried seaweed (I like Mara Seaweed's dulse; you will need a 10g sachet)

1 medium egg, beaten

Artichoke heart and thyme bread

Be sure to buy the artichoke hearts in a good quality olive oil, as you are incorporating the oil into the bread dough (or just use a couple of tablespoons of extra virgin olive oil instead).

Serve for lunch with perhaps a delicious herby and mango chicken salad or a feta and roasted sweet potato salad.

Place the flour and salt in a bowl, stir in the yeast and make a well in the centre.

Measure out 2 tablespoons of oil from the jar (or use extra virgin olive oil) and pour in, with about 275ml of tepid water. Combine to a firm dough, adding a splash or two extra of water if needed to bring it all together.

Gather up the dough in floured hands and knead on a floured board for 10 minutes (or in a mixer with a dough hook) until it feels smooth. Place it in a lightly oiled bowl, cover and leave somewhere vaguely warm for about 1½ hours until well risen.

Lightly oil a swiss-roll tin (23 × 33cm).

Knock back the dough by punching it with your fists, then press into the oiled tin, easing the dough out to the edges with your hands. Form a border all around by pressing the dough up the sides a little.

Mix the soured cream and egg together, season well with salt and pepper and pour this over the base, leaving the raised edges clear. Remove the artichokes from the jar, pat well dry, then slice thinly. Place these over the soured cream mixture. Scatter the finely chopped thyme on top and leave the tin somewhere vaguely warm for about 45 minutes or until the edges look puffy.

Preheat the oven to 220°C.

Bake for about 20 minutes or until it is well risen and golden. Leave to cool for at least 20 minutes before cutting into slices.

Makes 1 loaf

•

500g strong white flour

1 tsp salt

7g sachet fast-action
dried yeast

jar of artichoke hearts in oil
(weight: about 285g)

275ml tepid water

150ml soured cream

1 egg

salt and freshly ground
black pepper, to season

2 tbsp fresh thyme leaves,
finely chopped

Focaccia

Makes 1 large focaccia

•

500g Italian 00 flour
(or strong white flour,
if you can't get 00)

7g sachet fast-action dried
yeast

1 rounded tsp salt

2 tbsp extra virgin olive oil

275ml tepid water

•

Toppings

a few sprigs of fresh rosemary

a handful of black olives,
stoned

1 tbsp extra virgin olive oil

sea salt

Who doesn't love a focaccia? Traditionally served in Liguria both flavoured and drizzled with olive oil, it can also be topped with rosemary or sweet onions. There are also sweet types of focaccia in other parts of Italy. One of the many variations I love is one that is stuffed with Taleggio cheese and ham. You can make this by dividing the dough into two and pushing half out into the tray then topping with about 150g diced Taleggio and about 100g good quality cooked ham. Top with the other half of the dough and leave for its second rise before baking as below.

Classically made with Italian 00 flour, this gives the authentic soft texture, but if you can't find it, then strong white flour is fine; the texture will, however, be slightly less tender.

When I competed in *MasterChef* in 1991, I baked a focaccia to go with my main course in the semi-final, which was sea bass with red pepper and basil sauce and a tomato concasse. Whether it was that or the walnut and quince tart for dessert, or the starter of home-made pasta with chicken livers and lemon, I don't know – but I somehow made it through to the final.

Make the bread dough by mixing the flour, yeast and salt in a large bowl (or a food mixer). Add 2 tablespoons of oil to 275ml of tepid water and pour into the flour, adding a little more tepid water, if necessary. You should have a softish dough that comes away from the sides easily.

Tip this onto a floured surface and knead for 10 minutes until smooth. Alternatively, knead with a dough hook in the mixer for 6–7 minutes.

Place the dough in a lightly oiled bowl, cover with cling film and place somewhere vaguely warm to rise for about 1½ hours.

Lightly oil a swiss-roll tin (23 × 33cm).

Punch down the dough and, using a rolling pin, lightly roll out to a rectangle about the size of the tray and ease it into the baking tray.

Cover loosely with oiled cling film and leave somewhere vaguely warm for about an hour or until almost doubled in size.

Preheat the oven to 200°C.

Using your fingers (not fingertips, the whole finger 'pad'), make indentations all over, regularly spaced, and pop an olive or tiny sprig of rosemary into each little hole. Drizzle with the olive oil, then sprinkle some sea salt over the top.

Bake in the preheated oven for 18–20 minutes or until well risen and golden brown. Remove to a wire rack and leave until barely warm before cutting into squares.

Naan bread

When I was at university at Dundee, a favourite place to eat out was the Gunga Din on Perth Road. As well as a newly found love of curries and fragrant basmati rice, this special treat initiated my love of naan bread.

The concept today – or to those of my children's generation, who were students in the early 2000s – of finding naan bread a novelty is frankly risible, as it's been part of the culinary scene in Indian restaurants for decades. But as a student in the mid to late 1970s, dunking great chunks of lightly charred flatbread into curry sauce and dal felt to me like the most exotic thing ever.

It also felt slightly risqué, as, prior to that, food – apart from fish and chips from newspaper – was eaten strictly with a fork and knife. Curry with naan was eaten with a fork and a hand charged with a hunk of bread. Of course, after I returned from my year out in France, where baguette was dunked into all manner of foods, the novelty was not quite the same. But there was still almost a sensual delight in the process of ripping off hunks of naan, then dunking them into a rich, spicy sauce. I still love it.

And though authentic naan bread is almost impossible to make at home in a domestic oven – it is baked traditionally in a very hot tandoor (a clay oven) – this simple recipe is fine as a substitute now and then, and indeed can also be a decent alternative to pitta bread.

Some recipes stipulate cooking under a high grill; I prefer a very hot oven.

You can sprinkle a teaspoon or so of nigella or cumin seeds into the dough, if you like. Also, once it is baked, you can brush the naan with some melted ghee and sprinkle some finely chopped fresh coriander on top before serving warm.

Makes 4

•

200g plain flour

200g strong white flour

2 tsp fast-action dried yeast

1 tsp salt

3 tbsp natural yoghurt (runny, not set)

200ml tepid water

Mix the flours and the yeast together with the salt, then make a well in the middle. Add in the yoghurt and 200ml of tepid water and stir well. Using your hands, combine into a dough. Either knead by hand on a floured board for 10 minutes until it is smooth, or knead in a mixer with the dough hook for about 5 minutes.

Place in a bowl, cover and leave somewhere vaguely warm (I use a wire rack over my heated kitchen floor) for a couple of hours until the dough has risen.

Meanwhile, preheat the oven to 240°C. Place two large baking sheets inside, as it heats.

Tip the dough onto a floured board and, using floured hands, divide into four. Using a floured rolling pin, roll each out into an oval or tear shape.

Remove the two hot baking sheets and slap two naan breads onto each. Bake for about 10 minutes or until nicely scorched, swapping the trays over halfway through.

Wrap the naans in a tea towel and serve warm.

Cornbread

Makes 1 loaf

•

200g fine polenta or (yellow) cornmeal

150g plain flour

2 tsp baking powder

2 tsp caster sugar

1 tsp salt

150ml milk

1 egg, beaten

50g butter, melted

•

Optional flavourings

50g mature cheddar, grated

2 rounded tbsp sweetcorn

1 tbsp fresh chillies, finely chopped

1 rounded tbsp fresh oregano, chopped

I had my first American cornbread in Santa Fe, New Mexico, where it was always served in the bread basket, with baguette, in restaurants. Though I liked it – it is so good with chilli or a stew – I found it far too sweet. Some recipes have 6 tablespoons of sugar to the amount of cornmeal and flour; here I have reduced this to a couple of teaspoons as, even though we Scots have inordinately sweet teeth, we usually like to separate our sweet from our savoury, and cornbread is in the savoury section always.

You can add flavourings such as chilli, oregano, sweetcorn or cheese as you wish. If I am making for the family, I usually just add cheese, as then the little ones also adore it.

In the US, a batch of cornbread is often baked simply to make a cornbread stuffing for Thanksgiving (in which case, the sugar is reduced slightly). Pieces of it are added to bacon, sausagemeat, celery, herbs and egg to make a chunky stuffing that is baked alongside the turkey.

Preheat the oven to 190°C.

Butter an 18cm square baking tin.

Tip the polenta, flour, baking powder, caster sugar and salt into a bowl and stir to combine.

Add a flavouring of your choice now, stirring in.

Mix the milk, egg and butter, then whisk, slowly adding it to the bowl. Combine as gently as possible.

Tip the mixture into the prepared tin and bake for about 25 minutes or until tinged golden brown – and a wooden cocktail stick inserted into the middle comes out clean.

Leave in the tin for about 10 minutes, then decant onto a wire rack to cool before cutting into squares.

Tapenade parmesan breadsticks

I went to the wonderful Edinburgh New Town Cookery School for an artisan bread course and in one fascinating day I learned so many basics about bread and yeast. One of the last recipes that the owner, Fiona Burrell, demonstrated for us was olive, herb and parmesan sticks.

I went home on the bus afterwards and every passenger raised their head from their phone as I passed, my bag full of breads wafting delicious yeasty aromas down the entire aisle. The olive breadsticks were still warm and the smell was ridiculously tempting. This recipe is reminiscent of them.

Place the flour, salt and yeast in a bowl and stir well.

Add about 200ml of tepid water – enough to bring it together as a dough. Knead by hand for 10 minutes or in the food mixer with the dough hook until smooth. Place in a lightly oiled bowl and cover with cling film, then leave in a vaguely warm place for about 1½ hours until well risen.

Sprinkle some semolina or polenta onto a large board and place the dough on top. Using a rolling pin, roll out to a large rectangle about 1cm thick.

Spread the tapenade all over, then sprinkle with parmesan.

Fold one third of the dough over into the centre then fold the other third on top – as Fiona told us, as if you are folding a sheet of A4 paper to go in an envelope. Seal the ends, then using a sharp knife cut into about 20 strips.

Line a baking tray with parchment paper.

Take each strip between two hands and twist it, each hand twisting in the opposite direction, while you pull and stretch a little to make it longer. Place the strips on the baking tray, cover loosely with cling film and leave somewhere vaguely warm for about 45 minutes.

Preheat the oven to 240°C.

Bake for about 10–12 minutes or until golden brown.

Cool on a wire rack.

Makes 20

•

350g strong white flour

1 tsp salt

7g sachet fast-action dried yeast

200ml tepid water

sprinkling of semolina or polenta flour

50g (approx.) or a couple of tbsp black tapenade

25g parmesan, grated

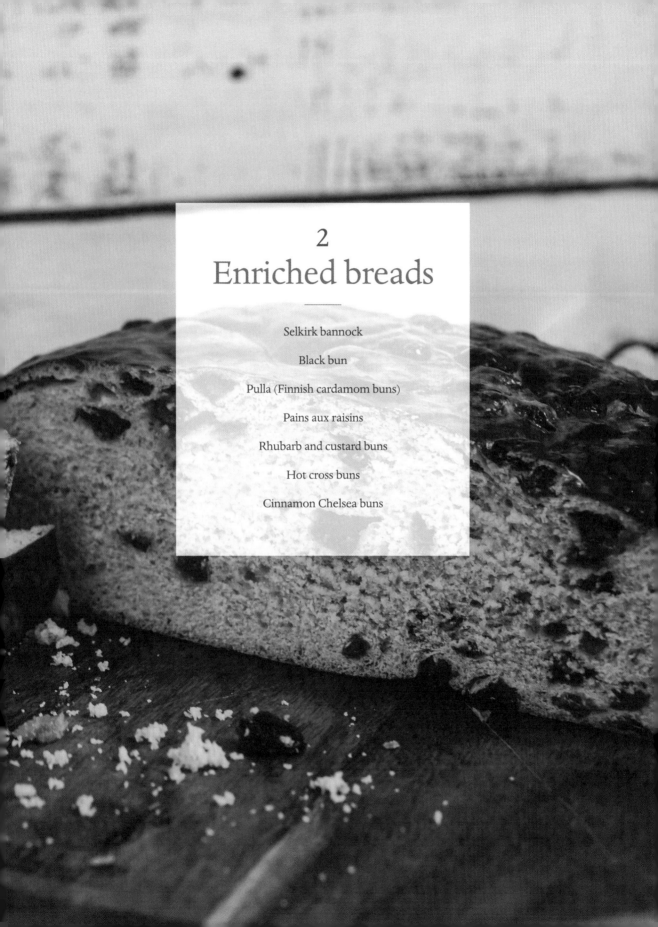

2
Enriched breads

Introduction

In times past in Scotland, no one apart from the wealthy had ovens – it was all about baking on the girdle (the Scots word for griddle). People could also take loaves along to the one village bakery and put them in a communal oven. Enriched breads were often made from leftover bread dough by adding butter, sugar and dried fruits. These made a delicious sweet offering for special occasions.

Across Scotland, these came in different forms, from Currie Birl in Shetland all the way south to Selkirk bannocks in the Borders. And don't forget traditional offerings such as black bun at Hogmanay; these used to be made with enriched bread dough, not pastry, as they are now.

Today, we have so many sweetened, enriched breads that they have become regular fare, whether a cinnamon roll or a Chelsea bun. Grab that flat white and enjoy!

Previous page: Selkirk bannock, p. 41
Below: Cinnamon Chelsea buns, p. 55

Selkirk bannock

Reputedly a favourite teatime treat of Queen Victoria, this rich fruited sweet bread is a speciality of the Borders, having originated in the town of Selkirk as a means of using up spare bread dough. Selkirk bannock lookalikes are made by bakers in other Borders towns, such as Galashiels, Hawick and Kelso. Bakers nowadays do not, of course, make them as a means of using up a batch of basic dough, then enriching it with butter, sugar and sultanas, but it is interesting to read the basic guidelines of this method in F. Marian McNeill's *The Scots Kitchen*:

> Get 2 pounds of dough from the baker. Into this rub 4 ounces of butter and 4 ounces of lard until melted but not oiled. Then work in ½ pound of sugar, ¾ pound sultanas and ¼ pound chopped orange peel. Put the dough into a buttered tin, let it stand for 30 minutes to rise then bake in a good steady oven.

Here is my more modern version (for those of us unable to buy 2lb of dough from the bakers!) for a magnificently bulging and moist bannock that is easy to make and all too easy to consume.

Mine is a lot less sweet than most traditional ones, which have some 200g of sugar, but I think the inherent sweetness of the dried fruit more than compensates. You can easily add an extra 25g of sugar, if you like. Also, since I am not keen on peel, I prefer to leave it out and use only sultanas. Besides, according to Theodora Fitzgibbon's *Taste of Scotland*, it was originally only made with the finest Turkish sultanas. I also like to add a hint of citrus by grating in some lemon zest.

It goes without saying that Selkirk bannock makes one of the most delicious bread and butter puddings, perhaps with a spreading of lemon curd or marmalade between each layer.

Halve the ingredients for a regular-sized bannock.

Add the flour, along with a pinch of salt, to a bowl, then rub in the butter till thoroughly combined. Stir in the yeast and sugar, then add the dried fruit and lemon zest.

Add enough of the tepid liquid to combine to a soft but not sticky dough. Bring together with lightly floured hands, then turn onto a floured board and knead well for 10 minutes or so until smooth. This is hard work with such a large mass of dough, but just think what it is doing for your upper arms!

Makes 1 large bannock

•

1kg strong white flour

pinch of salt

175g butter, softened

2 × 7g sachet fast-action dried yeast

75g caster sugar

500g sultanas and raisins (or just sultanas)

grated zest of 1 lemon (optional)

500ml (approx.) tepid milk and water, mixed

1 egg yolk, beaten, to glaze

Place in a lightly oiled bowl, cover and leave somewhere vaguely warm (I place my bowl on a wire rack over my heated kitchen floor) for about 2 hours, or until well risen.

Butter a baking sheet.

Shape the dough into a bannock – a round, flattened dome about 28cm in diameter – then place on the baking sheet and brush all over with half the egg yolk. Leave for about an hour, or until well risen.

Preheat the oven to 220°C.

Re-brush with the remaining yolk and bake for 10 minutes, then cover loosely with foil to prevent any fruit that is poking out from becoming burned; reduce the heat to 190°C and continue to bake for about 30 minutes.

It is ready once it's golden brown all over and the base sounds hollow when tapped. Leave to cool on a wire rack, then once completely cold, slice and spread with butter.

Black bun

Serves 12 – 16

•

For the pastry

280g plain flour

½ tsp baking powder

grated zest and juice of
1 lemon

150g unsalted butter, diced

3 – 4 tbsp cold water

1 medium egg, beaten,
to glaze

•

For the filling

450g raisins

600g currants

100g whole almonds, roughly
chopped

50g walnuts, roughly chopped

150g plain flour

75g caster sugar

1 tsp ground allspice

1 tsp ground ginger

1 tsp ground cinnamon

½ tsp cream of tartar

½ tsp baking powder

2 tbsp whisky

4 tbsp (approx.) milk

> There were stacks of Scots Bun, a dense black substance inimical to life, and full moons of shortbread adorned with peel or sugar plum in honour of the season and the family's affections.

This wonderful picture of a traditional Scottish festive table is from Robert Louis Stevenson's *Edinburgh: Picturesque Notes*, published in 1878. Although it is not one of my favourite bakes, I do not agree that black bun is 'inimical'. Though I can understand that the potential malevolence of the black inners of this shiny golden pastry case might be off-putting to some black bun virgins.

In our house at Hogmanay there were some things that never changed. The home-made blackcurrant cordial might have been replaced by Advocaat and lemonade as we became older, but there was always the tall dark man (my father) at the door at midnight with a piece of coal as the 'first foot' of the year, and there was always black bun.

Offered alongside the plate of shortbread with wedges of cheddar cheese and sultana or cherry cake, black bun – rich, heavy and dense – was perfect to soak up the copious amounts of whisky proffered in every household. ('Just one more dram before you go…') Black bun and 'shortie' were de rigueur everywhere, as we did the rounds of neighbours' houses first-footing until the wee small hours.

Black bun was supposedly the original Twelfth Night cake eaten in Scotland, before it became known as 'Scotch Christmas bun' during the first half of the nineteenth century. There is a recipe for a bun in Meg Dods' book, *The Cook and Housewife's Manual* (1929). It was traditionally a spiced fruit mixture encased in a bread dough, but the bread dough gradually gave way over the decades to the lighter shortcrust pastry case and the name became simply black bun.

Although raisins, sultanas and currants are often interchangeable, here you must ensure the majority of dried fruit is currants, for their black colour.

In Shetland, there is a traditional bake called Curnie Birl, a spiced fruit loaf encased in pastry. It is not dissimilar to black bun, but a little lighter. The 'birl' part refers to the shape – it has a swirl of pastry throughout, having been rolled up in a spiral. 'Birl' in Scots means to turn round and round or whirl about.

For the pastry, add the flour and baking powder to a bowl, then stir in the lemon zest. Rub in the butter, then add the lemon juice and 3 – 4 tablespoons of cold water – enough to bind it to a stiff dough. Turn out onto a lightly floured board and roll out thinly.

Butter a square 23cm loaf tin.

Use two-thirds of the pastry to line the base and sides of the tin. Roll out the remaining pastry to fit as a lid, cover and chill both the lid and the case for half an hour or so.

Preheat the oven to 140°C.

For the filling, mix everything together, except the whisky and milk. I do this with my hands – it is easier. Now add the whisky, and enough milk to moisten the mixture. Turn into the pastry case and press down well.

Dampen the top edges of the pastry all round with a little water and place the rolled-out pastry lid on top. Press together the edges to seal, then cut off any remaining pastry. Prick all over with a fork. Using a very thin skewer, prick right through to the base of the tin: 6–8 pricks altogether. Brush the surface with some beaten egg, retaining a little for later.

Bake for 2–2½ hours until golden brown on top, re-glazing with the remaining beaten egg after 1 hour of baking.

Cool in the tin for at least 2 hours, then carefully decant onto a wire rack to cool completely. Wrap in foil and store in an airtight container for at least 1 month – but for anything up to 3–4 months.

Pulla (Finnish cardamom buns)

These buns, called pulla, are as commonplace in Finland as scones are in Scotland. I came to adore them during my year out in north Finland after university. In every house you visited, you were offered pulla. They are essentially cardamom-flavoured yeasted bread buns served with coffee – or, when freshly baked, with a glass of ice-cold milk.

Cardamom is an everyday spice in Finland, having been imported into the country since the sixteenth century.

The basic recipe is used in many ways. The buns here are called *korvapuustit*. The dough can also be stretched into a swiss-roll tin, topped with lingonberries or blueberries mixed with sugar, and baked as a delicious berry pie. This is called *isoaidin pulla*, or Grandmother's pulla.

_____

Place the flour, sugar, yeast and salt in a bowl and combine well. Rub in the butter and stir in the crushed cardamom seeds.

Make a well in the centre and pour in the milk, bringing the mixture together with a spoon. Combine with your hands to form a dough.

Turn onto a floured surface and knead for about 10 minutes or until smooth. Place in a lightly oiled bowl, cover with cling film and leave to rise in a vaguely warm place for 2 – 3 hours.

Place 18 – 20 paper cases on a baking sheet (or on two, if you don't have a large baking sheet).

Knock back the dough, then gently roll with a rolling pin (or press out gently with the heels of your hand) to make a rectangle about 28 × 38cm.

Now make the filling. Spread the dough with the softened butter, then sprinkle over the sugar and finally the cinnamon.

Roll up, swiss-roll style, along the long side, to make a roly-poly. Cut into 18 – 20 slices. Place these, cut-side up, in the paper cases, close together. Cover loosely with cling film and leave to rise for 30 – 40 minutes.

Preheat the oven to 220°C.

Once risen, using your index fingers press down on the centre of each bun, so the spiral-like dough bulges upwards. Brush with beaten egg and bake for about 10 minutes or until golden brown.

Transfer to a wire rack to cool, then eat warm.

Makes 18 – 20

•

500g strong white flour

25g caster sugar

7g sachet fast-action dried yeast

1 tsp salt

75g butter, diced

2 tsp cardamom seeds (black seeds removed from the green pods and crushed well)

300ml tepid milk

•

For the filling

75g butter, softened

75g light muscovado sugar

2 tsp ground cinnamon

1 medium egg, beaten

Pains aux raisins

Makes 16

•

For the crème pâtissière

3 egg yolks

75g caster sugar

25g plain flour

300ml whole milk

half a fat vanilla pod, or 1 tsp
vanilla bean paste

•

For the dough

400g strong white flour

1 tsp salt

225g butter

25g caster sugar

7g sachet fast-action dried
yeast

250ml tepid milk/water (I use
half and half)

•

For the filling and topping

125g raisins

1 egg yolk, beaten

I absolutely adore pains aux raisins. If we are staying in a house in France and someone – usually me, in fact – is taking orders for the *boulangerie* run for breakfast and the day's baguettes, I always order a pain aux raisins. It's not that I don't like croissants and pains au chocolat – who doesn't? – it's just that the pain aux raisins and I have a special relationship.

It's clearly not something I knew as a child, as a Dundonian growing up in Edinburgh. Nor is it something I became acquainted with during my year out from university in Lourdes as *assistante*, or summers as an au pair in Arles, or as a student in Caen or Montpellier in the 1970s. But ever since the 1990s, when we started going to France with the children, it's been my morning treat.

It's a family joke that when in France I far too often join the queue at the village's one and only *boulangerie* to find that the last pain aux raisins is being sold to the woman just in front of me. I try not to sob. Back home, when we take our grandchildren to Edinburgh cafés for a babycino and a cheese scone, I often opt for a pain aux raisins instead, unless, as often seems to happen, the man in front has just ordered the last one. While I seriously consider asking him if he really, really wants it . . . a restraining hand is usually placed on my shoulder. My husband can read my thoughts.

Some pains aux raisins are simply a sweetened enriched bread dough; others are more of a croissant or Danish pastry dough. My recipe is a variation on the latter. My methods are neither traditional nor authentic, so don't write in if I have omitted one essential quarter turn or double fold; this recipe works well for me and hopefully will for you too.

Feel free to add flavouring, such as a half teaspoon of ground cinnamon or some grated orange zest sprinkled over the raisins before you roll up the dough. You can also soak the raisins first in 3–4 tablespoons of rum for a couple of hours, then drain them well before scattering over the crème pâtissière. You can also glaze or ice them once baked: heat some apricot jam with a splash of water, then brush this over the top once they emerge from the oven, or drizzle over some glacé icing once they are baked and cooled.

First, make the crème pâtissière: place the yolks, sugar and flour in a bowl with 1 tablespoon of the measured milk. Using a balloon whisk, beat until combined and thick.

Place the milk in a saucepan. If using a vanilla pod, cut in half lengthways and scrape out the tiny black seeds. Add these – or the vanilla bean paste – to the milk and bring it slowly to the boil.

Remove from the heat whenever you see bubbles. Whisking all the time, pour this hot milk slowly over the egg mixture. Whisk until combined, then tip the contents back into the saucepan and heat gently, whisking continuously for about 2 – 3 minutes until thickened and smooth. Remove from the heat and spoon into a bowl. Cover the surface closely with cling film (to prevent a skin forming) and chill well until required.

For the dough, place the flour and salt in a bowl. Dice 25g of butter and rub it into the flour until it resembles breadcrumbs. Stir in the sugar and yeast, then add enough of the tepid liquid to combine to a soft dough. You may not need all the liquid.

Knead with a dough hook for about 7 – 8 minutes or by hand for 10 minutes until the dough is smooth and elastic. Ease out the dough to form a rough rectangle shape (this makes for easy rolling later), wrap in cling film and chill (in the fridge) for 1 – 1½ hours.

The remaining 200g of butter should be left at room temperature while the dough chills. If it's a warm day, however, pop it in the fridge. It has to be rolled out, so should be pliable but not soft.

After the dough's chilling time is up, place the block of butter between two large sheets of cling film and roll it out with a rolling pin to a rectangle about 30 × 20cm.

Remove the dough from the fridge and place it on a large, lightly floured board. Roll it out to a rectangle of about 50 × 25cm.

Now place the butter in the centre of the dough (positioned so you can fold in the two sides). Fold over each uncovered side of dough, so each side of dough is covering half of the butter; the side flaps will now meet in the middle. Using your fingers, seal the edges by pinching together. Clingwrap and chill again for 20 – 30 minutes.

Return the dough to the floured board, again with the seam down the middle, then give it a turn so the seam is now along the length of the dough. Roll out to make a rectangle, again about 50 × 25cm. Then make a simple fold by folding over the right-hand third of dough into the middle. Then fold the left-hand third over this, so you now have a three-layered dough sandwich. Cover with cling film and chill again for 20 – 30 minutes.

(At this stage, you can repeat the rolling and folding after giving the dough a quarter turn, chilling afterwards again. I personally think that the results are excellent with just one lot of folding into the three-layered dough sandwich, but if you have time, then feel free to do another roll and chill.)

Remove the dough from the fridge and place on a lightly floured board. Roll out again, till you have a rectangle about 50 × 25cm. The long edge should be nearest you, the two short edges to your right and left. Spread most of the crème pâtissière over the whole rectangle, ensuring you keep a border around the edges of about 2cm. You won't need all the crème pâtissière; you'll have a tablespoon or so left. Cook's perks!

Scatter over the raisins, evenly. Then, starting from the long edge furthest away, using both hands, roll the dough towards you in a long sausage shape, keeping the roll as tight as possible (but without squishing out the filling.)

Line two baking sheets with parchment paper.

Using a sharp knife, cut the dough in half, then halve this again, and so on, until you have 16 slices. (It is more reliable cutting in halves, then quarters, eighths, etc., than simply slicing from one end.)

Place these on the two baking sheets, ensuring they are spaced apart. Cover loosely with cling film and leave somewhere warm (I place mine on a wire rack over my heated kitchen floor) for 1½ – 2 hours, or until they have almost trebled in size.

Meanwhile, preheat the oven to 200°C.

Once they are well risen, remove the cling film and, using forefinger and thumb, tuck the end piece of each underneath (this ensures they don't un-spiral as they bake). Mix the egg yolk with a splash or two of water and use this to glaze the tops and sides of each pain aux raisins.

Bake for about 15 – 20 minutes, or until golden brown, swapping trays halfway if both trays are in the same oven. Remove and leave to cool for 5 minutes or so on their trays before removing to a board to cool. Dive in while still warm and think how lucky you are for once to be first in the queue . . . Smug face is permitted.

Rhubarb and custard buns

These are very easy to make, ideally with fresh rhubarb, though if it's out of season you can use frozen (but ensure it is really well patted dry first). Try to find the glorious thin, bright pink rhubarb from early in the season; if thick, cut in half lengthways.

Instead of the rhubarb, you could use a couple of brambles/blackberries in each bun, if they are in season.

For the dough, place the flour, sugar, yeast, ginger and a good pinch of salt in a large bowl. Rub in the butter, then make a well in the centre and slowly add the milk, bringing the mixture together with a large spoon. Combine to a dough with your hands.

Tip onto a floured board and knead for about 10 minutes or until smooth.

Place in a lightly oiled bowl, cover with cling film and leave it somewhere vaguely warm for about 3 hours – or until well risen. (I place a wire rack over my heated floor and put the bowl on that so it is not directly touching the heat source.)

Preheat the oven to 220°C. Place ten large paper bun/muffin cases on a baking tray.

Knock back the dough and gently roll it out to a rectangle about 25 × 35cm.

Sprinkle over the ginger, then roll it up, swiss-roll style, along the long edge to make a roly-poly.

Cut into ten slices and place these, cut side up, in the paper cases. Using your index finger, press down into the centre of each bun to form a shallow dip. Cover loosely in cling film and leave somewhere warm for 30–40 minutes or until risen.

Once risen, press down again to ensure there is a shallow indent in the middle, then fill each with 1 rounded teaspoon of custard, then place 2–3 pieces of rhubarb on top. Sprinkle each with some demerara sugar, then bake in the oven for 12–14 minutes or until puffed up and golden brown. Eat warm or cold.

Makes 10

•

450g strong white flour

25g caster sugar

7g sachet fast-action dried yeast

1 tsp ground ginger

good pinch of salt

75g butter, diced

250ml tepid milk

•

For the topping

1 tsp ground ginger

4 tbsp (approx.) thick custard (you can use a tub or packet)

100–150g rhubarb, trimmed, cut into small pieces

sprinkle of demerara sugar

Hot cross buns

Makes 12

•

500g strong white flour

1 tsp salt

50g butter, diced

40g light muscovado sugar

½ tsp mixed spice

½ tsp ground cinnamon

100g raisins and currants

25g chopped mixed peel
(optional)

7g sachet fast-action
dried yeast

300ml (approx.) tepid
milk/water (for this, I use
two-thirds whole milk,
one-third water)

•

For the crosses

3 rounded tbsp plain flour

2–3 tbsp cold water

or

70g plain flour

40g butter, diced

1–2 tbsp cold water

•

For the glaze

1 tbsp golden syrup or honey

Traditionally served on Good Friday with the symbolic cross on top, this is an easy recipe that can be varied, depending on personal likes and dislikes. One of the very few things I am not keen on is mixed peel, so I leave it out, but if you like it then add it along with the other dried fruit.

For the crosses, you can either make a thick floury paste and pipe it, or make pastry and lay it across the buns. I usually favour the second method, as I am not known for my proficiency with a piping bag. Tara Heron, who runs the brilliant micro-bakery Dainty Monkey in Trinity, Edinburgh, uses strong flour for the crosses for her deliciously spiced buns. For 12 buns, she mixes 50g strong white flour with 50ml water and 10ml olive oil. She leaves this rather thick mixture to sit for an hour or two before piping it onto the buns with a piping syringe.

Eat warm, just as they are – or cold with a tiny smear of butter, freshly baked. After a couple of days, they are wonderful split and toasted.

Nowadays you can buy insane-sounding flavours of hot cross buns, from chocolate orange or sticky toffee to goat's cheese and honey. And though I am more of a purist when it comes to these Easter treats, I was fascinated to learn from our family friends on Bermuda about Easter traditions there. As well as flying kites on Good Friday, they also eat fish cakes in hot cross buns. Made from salt cod, the fish cakes are placed inside the bun and devoured, usually on a delightfully warm Bermuda spring day on one of that island's fabulous pink sandy beaches. So, weird though it sounds, I know how delightful it must be.

Place the flour in a bowl, then stir in the salt. Rub in the butter until it resembles breadcrumbs.

Stir in the sugar, spices and dried fruits (and peel, if using), then stir in the yeast.

Slowly mix in the tepid liquid, then bring it together in your hands to a ball. You may need a splash or two more liquid to combine it in your hands; the dough should be soft but not sticky. Turn out onto a floured board and knead for about 10 minutes until springy and rather smooth. Once it is kneaded enough, place in a lightly oiled bowl and cover. Leave to rise somewhere vaguely warm for about 2½ – 3 hours or until risen. Houses vary in temperature – my dough takes a minimum of 2½ hours till it is risen, with an enriched dough like this. Test if it is ready for shaping by gently pressing a finger onto the dough. If it leaves an indentation, it is ready.

Line a baking sheet with parchment paper.

Knock back the dough and divide into 12 pieces, each weighing approximately 100g. Roll into balls, tucking the edges under and trying to ensure the dried fruit is not protruding (it will burn), then place them on the baking sheet, side by side (I like to pull them apart so you end up with soft, fluffy edges; if you prefer individual buns, then leave space between them). Score a cross across the top of each bun. Cover loosely and place somewhere vaguely warm for about an hour or until risen again (remember that enriched bread dough takes longer to rise).

Preheat the oven to 220°C.

For the piped crosses, mix the plain flour with enough cold water to make a thick paste. Using a piping bag (or a plastic freezer bag with a small hole, about 1cm, snipped in the corner), pipe a line over each row of buns, then turn the tray and repeat in the other direction to create crosses.

For the pastry crosses, place the flour in a bowl and rub in the butter, then add enough cold water to combine into a stiff dough. Break into 24 pieces and roll out (as if you were rolling plasticine between the palms of your hands). Join two together to form a cross, and place one over each risen bun.

Bake in the preheated oven for about 20 minutes or until golden brown and cooked through.

While they are baking, gently melt the syrup or honey (I do this in a microwave).

When they are ready, remove from the oven, lift them onto a wire rack and brush the tops of each with the glaze, then cool.

Cinnamon Chelsea buns

Who doesn't love a Chelsea bun? You see them everywhere, from traditional bakeries to hip cafés all over the country.

The Chelsea buns from Fitzbillies in Cambridge are legendary – they are the most glorious, stickiest bun ever. When you read their recipe, you see why: there is a huge amount of golden syrup brushed all over them. My recipe is slightly less extravagant, but hopefully almost as delicious.

Most traditional recipes have only currants, or mainly currants, but I prefer a mixture of sultanas, raisins and currants.

Combine the flour, cinnamon and salt in a large bowl.

Rub in the butter until it resembles breadcrumbs. Then stir in the yeast.

Whisk together the sugar and egg, then add most of the tepid milk. Pour this into the dry ingredients, adding extra tepid milk if necessary, so it comes together as a rough dough. Turn onto a lightly floured board and knead for about 10 minutes or until it feels smooth. Place the dough in a lightly oiled bowl and cover with cling film. Place somewhere vaguely warm for about 2–3 hours or until risen.

Tip the dough onto a floured board and roll out to a rectangle about 36 × 26cm.

Butter a square 23cm-deep baking tin.

For the topping, melt the butter. Using a pastry brush, brush all over the rectangle. Mix the dried fruits together with the sugar and sprinkle evenly over the butter, leaving a border on the long side furthest away from you. Carefully roll the dough towards you, as if rolling a swiss roll. Poke any wayward fruit back in. Press the joins gently together to seal.

Using a sharp knife, cut into nine even-sized pieces. Arrange them in the tin, cut side up, so you can see the pinwheel of fruit. The pieces should be touching but not too tightly squashed together. Cover loosely with cling film and place somewhere vaguely warm for about 45 minutes or until puffed up.

Preheat the oven to 200°C.

Once the buns are risen, bake them for about 25 minutes or until golden brown.

Warm the honey (I do this in the microwave for a couple of turns), then brush the tops using a pastry brush. Leave in the tin for 5 minutes or so, then carefully remove to a wire rack to cool. Lever them out using two large fish slices.

After 10–15 minutes of cooling, pull the buns apart.

Makes 9

•

450g strong white flour

2 tsp ground cinnamon

½ tsp salt

50g butter, diced

7g sachet fast-action dried yeast

25g caster sugar

1 medium egg

225g (approx.) tepid milk

•

For the topping

40g butter

50g raisins

50g currants

50g sultanas

50g light muscovado sugar

1 tbsp clear honey

3
Scones, pancakes & oatcakes

Fruit scones

Cheese scones

Buttermilk scones

Aga scones

Treacle scones

Shona's apricot and coconut scones

Apple scones

Scotch pancakes

Potato scones

Girdle scones

Soda farls

Sauty bannocks

Fairy butter

Fatty cutties

Sour scones

Beremeal bannocks

Oatcakes

Cheesy oatcakes

Seeded oatcakes

Introduction

Scones were pretty much an everyday occurrence when I was young. Whether it was a treacle scone, a fruit scone or a plain scone, they were just always there, ready to be split and buttered. And because of our renowned sweet tooth in Scotland, there was also always jam.

Jam or jelly (my mum's blackcurrant jelly was a great favourite) was also served on buttered pancakes. We didn't call them Scotch pancakes or drop scones, they were just pancakes, whose resemblance to a French crêpe is purely in the fact they are both made with a batter consisting of eggs, milk and flour.

Oatcakes have been part of Scotland's culinary offering for centuries. In the old days, travellers and soldiers journeyed with a bag of oatmeal and a girdle (the Scots word for griddle) to make them on the road. Simple and nutritious, oatcakes are quintessentially Scottish – and infinitely versatile.

SCONE TIPS

- When making scones, use the lightest touch possible. If you knead vigorously, you develop the gluten and end up with a tough scone. So handle the dough as little as possible.
- All scones taste better warm, though never hot. They should always be eaten on the day they are made. On the off chance there are some left over, freeze them, then reheat them another day from frozen in a loose foil parcel in a medium oven.
- You can use sweet scones as a pudding topping, in dishes like a cobbler: place 6–8 uncooked plain scones onto a dish of poached stewed fruit (plums, brambles, rhubarb, etc.) and bake at 230°C for 15–20 minutes until golden. Serve this delicious hot pudding with ice cream or thick yoghurt.
- Substituting buttermilk for milk in any scone recipe makes it nicely moist, almost spongey. Instead of 150ml milk, you need a little more (about 200ml) buttermilk.
- The wetter the scone mix, the more successful your scones will be, but do not overdo the liquid or they will spread out sideways instead of rising elegantly upwards.
- Scones are often glazed to enhance their appearance. The simplest way is to brush with milk, but a beaten egg gives a lovely golden crust, though they can become too dark in a very hot oven. Try to ensure none of the glaze drips down the side, otherwise the scone will tilt towards the drip.
- Scone etiquette demands that instead of slicing your scone open horizontally, you gently tear it apart with both hands. It is possibly because the tender crumb inside will be ruined by a harsh metal knife sawing through, but the main reason I do it is that, weirdly, it's incredibly satisfying. It gives two more or less even halves ready for you to spread thickly with butter or cream and jam.

Previous page: Shona's apricot and coconut scones, p. 67

Fruit scones

This basic scone is incredibly versatile. You can substitute currants for sultanas, or add 40g of dark chocolate chips and the crushed seeds from 2–3 cardamom pods for a change. Or you can try a rounded tablespoon of desiccated coconut and the zest of a small lemon, adding a splash more milk to bind. You can also omit all flavourings and serve a satisfyingly simple plain scone.

Lightly butter a baking tray. Preheat the oven to 220°C.

Mix the flour and baking powder in a large bowl and add a pinch of salt. Rub in the butter, then stir in the sugar and sultanas.

Lightly whisk the eggs in a measuring jug and add enough milk to bring the liquid up to 300ml.

Slowly add this to the dry ingredients, then very gently combine, first with a spoon or palette knife, then finally get in with floured hands to shape it into a round. Place this on a floured board. Pat out gently to about 3cm, then using a large floured cutter divide the round into 8 scones, or using a smaller one into 12.

Place them on the baking tray and brush the tops with any leftover egg/milk (or add a splash more milk), then bake near the top of the preheated oven for about 12 minutes or until well risen and golden.

Leave to cool on a wire rack.

Makes 8 large or
12 small scones

•

450g plain flour

2 rounded tbsp baking powder

pinch of salt

125g butter, diced

40g caster sugar

75g sultanas

2 eggs

150ml (approx.) milk

Cheese scones

Makes 8 large or
12 small scones

•

450g plain flour

2 rounded tbsp baking powder

125g butter, diced

250g mature cheddar, grated
(plus extra for sprinkling
on top)

pinch of salt

a twist of cracked black pepper
(optional)

2 eggs

150ml (approx.) milk

We have taken our grandchildren out to cafés for a babycino and a cheese scone since the eldest, Matilda, was little – and we soon discovered there can be a huge variation in the taste of a cheese scone. Some can be rather leaden, some lacking in cheese, some bizarrely sweet – and some clearly not baked that day. But most are light, superbly cheesy and still a little warm from the oven.

This recipe is based on the one from Fi MacInnes, chef and owner of Porto & Fi, a brilliant café in Newhaven overlooking the sea in Edinburgh. She sometimes adds paprika to the mix, or sprinkles the scones with poppy seeds just before baking. You can also add a little dry mustard powder or cayenne pepper to the mix for a nice kick – though I find that is more for an afternoon with a cup of tea, rather than morning coffee. Or add some finely chopped herbs (chives, thyme or oregano are good) with the milk/egg and serve them with a bowl of soup at lunch.

You can also cut them into tiny little rounds and serve them, as canapés, split and topped with cream cheese or soft goat's cheese and then a sliver of smoked salmon or roasted red pepper.

You can also top each scone with a spoonful of thick cheese sauce just before going into the oven for a gloriously blistered, gooey crust.

Infinitely versatile, these are ever present in my freezer in case a cheese scone emergency occurs.

Lightly butter a baking tray. Preheat the oven to 220°C.

Add the flour and baking powder to a large bowl, then rub in the butter. Stir in the cheese, then add a pinch of salt and the pepper (if using).

Place the eggs in a measuring jug, whisk lightly, then add enough milk to bring it up to 300ml. Stir, then add most of this to the mix (enough to make to a softish dough). Gently combine, getting stuck in with your floured hands. Bring together gently (you do not need to knead, only bring the dough together with a light touch) and place on a floured surface, then pat out till about 3cm high. Using a fluted cutter, cut out the scones and place on the buttered baking tray.

Brush the tops with any liquid left in the jug (add a splash more milk, if necessary), then top with the extra cheese. Bake near the top of the oven for about 12 minutes or until golden and well risen.

Remove to a wire rack and leave until barely warm before halving and spreading with butter.

Buttermilk scones

Makes 10 small or
8 medium scones

•

250g self-raising flour

pinch of salt

50g butter, diced

2 tsp caster sugar

1 small egg

150ml buttermilk, stirred

These are based on the traditional Scottish oven scone, made with plain flour, bicarbonate of soda, cream of tartar – and buttermilk. I often prefer the ease of self-raising flour, but don't forego the buttermilk and substitute with fresh milk, as there is a slight tang and a welcome moistness when made with buttermilk.

Made in a flash, these can be rustled up if a friend messages to say they are popping over in half an hour. And if you leave out the sugar, they can be served with a bowl of soup and some good cheese for lunch.

Butter a baking sheet. Preheat the oven to 220°C.

Place the flour in a bowl with a pinch of salt. Rub in the butter until it resembles breadcrumbs, add the sugar then make a well in the centre. Add the egg and buttermilk, then, using a table knife, bring it all together. With floured hands, gently combine to a dough. It is very soft but you must use the lightest touch possible.

Press out to a thickness of about 2.5cm, then, using a floured cutter, cut into scones and place on the baking sheet. Dust lightly with flour, then bake for 10 – 12 minutes or until risen and golden brown.

Aga scones

The same rules apply with Aga scones as for the regular variety: have a wettish, almost sticky mixture and handle as little – and as lightly – as you can. Baking scones in an Aga, however, is even quicker than making regular scones since, of course, the oven is already on. So all you need is, say, 3–4 minutes to prepare and 10 minutes to bake.

Lightly butter a baking sheet.

Mix the flour, baking powder and a pinch of salt in a bowl, then rub in the butter until it resembles breadcrumbs. Stir in the sugar, then add enough milk to make a softish dough. Bring together with floured hands and place on a floured board.

Pat out gently to a height of about 2.5cm, then cut with a fluted or plain cutter into 6–8 scones and place onto the baking sheet.

Slide the shelf onto the third set of runners in the roasting oven and place the baking tray on top. Bake for about 10 minutes or until just cooked. Remove to a wire rack to cool, then eat warm.

Makes 6–8

•

225g self-raising flour

1 tsp baking powder

pinch of salt

50g butter, diced

25g caster sugar

175–200ml milk

Treacle scones

Makes 8 – 10

•

300g self-raising flour

½ tsp baking powder

50g butter, diced

½ tsp ground cinnamon

½ tsp ground ginger

pinch of mixed spice

25g caster sugar

2 tbsp black treacle

175g buttermilk,
plus extra to glaze

I have always loved treacle puddings and any baked goods involving black treacle. Treacle scones were part of my mother's regular home-baking repertoire when I was young; black treacle was always hugely popular in Scotland, whether in steamed puddings, gingerbread or scones.

The other type of treacle scones I had as a child appeared at Halloween. Then we would attempt to bite thick, floury triangular scones daubed in sticky black treacle. The snag was that they were hung on a string from the washing line in the kitchen and our hands were tied behind our backs. Thankfully, the next game was always dooking for apples, which involved full facial immersion in tubs of freezing cold water. I always preferred Halloween parties where you could balance with a fork in your mouth to spear the apple instead of plunging your head into the tub of bobbing apples.

My mum's treacle scone recipe was simple, with treacle added and some ground ginger. Delicious though they were, they were never the lightest, probably because of the heavy black treacle. So when I saw Judy Murray tweet a picture of afternoon tea at Cromlix Hotel in Perthshire, owned by her son Andy, I zoomed into the bottom tier of the cake stand. Those treacle scones looked so light. Cromlix Hotel kindly sent me their recipe, which uses buttermilk, and I am sure that's what helps the lightness and good rise.

This recipe is a combination of Mum's and theirs. Eat warm with butter.

Butter a baking tray. Preheat the oven to 220°C.

Place the flour and baking powder in a bowl and rub in the butter until it resembles breadcrumbs. Stir in the three spices and the sugar.

Place the treacle in a microwave-proof bowl and heat briefly until just warm, not hot. It is to make the treacle liquid, not to heat it through. You can also heat it in a saucepan.

Using a whisk, gradually add the buttermilk to the treacle, whisking until thick and creamy and the treacle is amalgamated into the buttermilk. Make a well in the middle of the flour mixture and slowly pour in the liquid, combining gently to a softish dough.

With lightly floured hands, bring the dough together, using a light touch and with minimal handling (otherwise the scones will be tough.) Pat out to a thickness of about 3cm with your hands. If there are any cracks, knead gently together to smooth them over. Using a scone cutter, cut out eight to ten scones. Place on the baking tray.

Place a tablespoon or so of buttermilk in a small dish and loosen it down with a splash of milk. Then, using a pastry brush, brush this over the tops of the scones. Bake in the oven for about 10 minutes or until well risen. Cool on a wire rack before eating, split and spread with butter.

Shona's apricot and coconut scones

One hot June morning in Shona MacIntyre's garden in Port Ellen, I enjoyed some of her delicious scones with tea. Butter and home-made jam to hand, we sat and caught up on all the Islay news. Soon, the sun was so strong the butter was melting, but the Islay hospitality went on. Another pot of tea made, another scone devoured, and it was only when the midges began hovering in the still, hot air that I dragged myself away.

Shona makes these scones either with chopped apricots or glacé cherries. Both look and taste delicious.

Butter a baking tray. Preheat the oven to 220°C.

Rub the butter into the flour until it resembles fine breadcrumbs, then stir in the sugar, coconut and dried apricots/cherries.

Make a well in the centre and add the egg and enough milk to bind – start with about 100ml then add more to give a soft but not sticky dough.

Gently combine on a floured board, then cut out and place on the baking tray.

Bake in the oven for about 12 minutes or until well risen. Remove to a wire rack and leave to cool a little before spreading with butter – and jam, if you like.

Makes 8

•

50g butter, diced

225g self-raising flour

25g caster sugar

50g desiccated coconut

50g dried apricots (or glacé cherries), chopped

1 egg

125ml (approx.) whole milk

Apple scones

Makes 10 small,
or 8 medium scones

•

250g self-raising flour

¼ tsp baking powder

50g butter, diced

25 – 50g demerara sugar

1 medium cooking apple
(approx. 200g unpeeled), peeled
and grated

150ml (approx.) buttermilk

These are delicious, moist scones whose flavour can be enhanced with the addition of a pinch of ground cloves or cinnamon, if you like a gentle hint of spice with your apple.

Cooking apples vary in their tartness, so add between 25g and 50g of sugar accordingly. The best way to assess is to taste the grated apple – if it's really tart, use 50g.

Butter a baking tray. Preheat the oven to 220°C.

Mix the flour and baking powder, then rub in the butter until it resembles breadcrumbs. Stir in the sugar, then the grated apple, and make a well in the centre. Add enough buttermilk to combine to a soft – yet not sticky – dough.

Pat out on a floured board with floured hands, then cut into scones with a cutter.

Place on the baking tray and bake in the oven for 12 – 15 minutes, or until risen and golden brown. Serve warm or cold with butter.

Scotch pancakes

'Scotch' pancakes to Sassenachs; simply 'pancakes' to Scots. They are also known as 'drop scones' down south, because the batter is loose enough to be dropped onto the girdle.

This is fast food as it was meant to be.

From mixing the ingredients for these pancakes to eating them warm, with a cup of tea, takes as little as 10 minutes. And what could be more delicious or easy than making pancakes to eat with butter and jam – either on a girdle or in a frying pan.

This is based on my mother's recipe, though Mum always used plain flour with cream of tartar and bicarbonate of soda instead of self-raising flour.

If you have never used a girdle before, it is easy: you can test it is hot enough by dropping a teaspoonful of the batter onto the surface. It should set almost at once, and if it begins to bubble after 1 minute, the girdle is hot enough. It is the large bubbles that tell you the pancakes are ready to be flipped over.

They are best eaten immediately after being made, but you can make a batch and freeze for some later date.

Makes 12 – 16

·

150g self-raising flour

¼ tsp bicarbonate of soda

pinch of salt

1 tbsp caster sugar

1 egg, beaten

175ml milk

a little butter, to cook

Add the first two ingredients into a bowl and add a pinch of salt. Stir in the sugar, then make a well in the middle.

Add the egg and, with a balloon whisk, bring together, gradually adding the milk, whisking all the time. Continue whisking until you have a smooth batter.

Preheat the girdle (or heavy-based frying pan) to medium. Using a piece of kitchen paper, smear it all over with a thin film of butter. Once it is hot (mine takes 4 – 5 minutes to heat up over a low heat) drop spoonfuls of batter onto the girdle, four at a time. If you want dainty little ones, use a dessertspoon; for slightly larger ones, use a tablespoon.

After about 1½ – 2 minutes you will notice large bubbles forming on the surface of each. Using a spatula, flip each one over and continue cooking for a further 1 – 1½ minutes until just done. (They should take about 3 – 3½ minutes altogether.) Continue with the remaining batter, re-smearing the girdle with a tiny amount of butter for each batch.

Remove and keep warm – I put them in a folded tea towel over a wire rack. Then serve with butter and jam.

Potato scones

Makes 8

•

1 large potato (about 250g)

25g butter

50g plain flour

½ tsp salt

¼ tsp baking powder

butter, to cook

Known more commonly throughout Scotland as tattie scones, these are a kind of girdle scone often served for breakfast or tea. Sometimes I add about 25g of grated cheddar or a tablespoon or so of finely chopped herbs (parsley or mint are good) to the mixture and serve them with a bowl of broth or lentil soup for lunch.

Eat them warm, with a thin smear of butter, whenever they are made. They can also be made in advance: just loosely wrap them in foil and reheat in a low oven. Leftovers can be toasted the next day.

Use a floury potato such as Maris Piper or King Edward. And though some recipes suggest using leftover (cold) mash, I don't think it works as well as freshly boiled and warm mashed potato, which absorbs the flour more evenly.

Interestingly, though we always cut them into quarters before cooking, F. Marian McNeill's recipe is for them to be cooked in rounds. Then, once baked, they are buttered and rolled up before being eaten.

Peel the potato, cut into chunks and cook in boiling water until tender, then drain well. Using a potato masher, mash the potato with the butter. Now weigh it: you need about 200g of mash.

Add the flour, salt and baking powder to a bowl. While the mash is still warm, stir it into the flour and combine well. Using lightly floured hands, gently shape this mixture into two balls and turn onto a lightly floured surface. With a rolling pin, roll out gently to form two circles about 5mm thick. Cut each circle into quarters. Prick all over with a fork.

Heat the girdle (or heavy-based frying pan) to medium-hot, smear over a little butter, then, once hot, transfer four scones to it with a large spatula or fish slice. Cook for about 3–4 minutes on each side until tinged with golden brown. Transfer to a wire rack to cool briefly before spreading with a little butter and eating warm.

Girdle scones

————

Makes 4 – 6

•

a little sunflower oil, to cook

250g self-raising flour

½ tsp bicarbonate of soda

½ tsp salt

2 tsp caster sugar

1 medium egg

25g butter, melted, cooled slightly

200ml buttermilk (or approx. 175ml milk)

These are traditionally baked on a girdle, but they can also be baked in the oven (200°C for 20–25 minutes). They are delicious split apart and smeared with butter and jam. They are also good with a hearty beef stew, in which case reduce the sugar to 1 teaspoon.

————

First, put on your girdle (or heavy-based frying pan) and heat to medium-hot, smearing with a little oil.

Add the flour and bicarbonate of soda to a bowl, along with the salt and the sugar. Make a well in the centre and add the egg, melted butter and enough buttermilk (or milk) to combine to a soft dough. Do not overwork.

Tip this onto a floured board and, using floured hands (it will be sticky), shape the dough into a round about 22cm in diameter and 2cm thick. Don't knead, just pat it gently into shape. Using a floured knife, cut into quarters or sixths. Dust lightly with flour and transfer carefully to the medium-hot girdle.

Cook for about 5 minutes – by which time the scones will have risen and formed a fabulous brown crust underneath – then carefully flip each one over. Reduce the heat to low and continue to cook until they're all done. They are ready when no liquid oozes out the sides if you press down lightly; the edges should be dry. It might take 15 minutes altogether, so 5 minutes first side, then 8 – 10 minutes on the other.

Transfer to a wire rack and serve warm.

Soda farls

On a warm, sunny summer's day on Islay, chef and broadcaster Paula McIntyre came over to visit on the *Kintyre Express* from Ballycastle. And as we gazed over to Northern Ireland from my garden, we discussed the similarities between traditional Scots and Ulster dishes. Potato (tattie) scones, called fadge, are common, as is cloutie dumpling. Girdle scones are called farls – the word 'farl' meaning quadrant, describing the shape the scones are cut into before cooking.

She brought me some delicious freshly baked soda farls and this is her recipe, one everyone in her family – and indeed all the neighbours – would have used. Her granny had an old goose wing that she used to dust the scorched flour off the griddle in between batches – since no one ever made just four, there were always about 20 made at one go.

Paula told me you can also add 2 tablespoons of black treacle to the buttermilk to make treacle farls. Or add 25g of raisins or sultanas to the mix for fruit 'slims': for these, divide the dough in half, roll each half into a round, only 1cm thick, and cut into six wedges.

Mix the flour with the bicarbonate of soda and the salt, then make a well in the centre. Add the buttermilk and mix to a soft dough.

Flour a surface and knead the dough gently into a ball, then flatten it to about 2cm thick. Cut into quarters (farls) and leave for 10 minutes.

Heat a large heavy-based frying pan or griddle (girdle in Scots, but Paula refers to it as griddle) over a medium heat. When hot, add the farls. Cook for about 5 minutes on each side or until they sound hollow when tapped. Paula insists you mustn't rush the farl; indeed, sometimes people turn them on their sides to ensure they're cooked through – this is called 'harning'.

Makes 4 large farls

·

350g plain flour

1½ tsp bicarbonate of soda

½ tsp salt

325ml buttermilk (or 325ml whole milk with 1½ tbsp of vinegar added)

Sauty bannocks

Makes 12

•

300ml milk

125g medium oatmeal

2 medium eggs, beaten

25g caster sugar

grating of nutmeg

grated zest of 1 lemon

½ tsp baking powder

pinch of salt

butter, to cook

The name sauty bannocks, from the French verb *sauter*, to jump or toss, is a nod to the Auld Alliance, which meant that before the Union of the Crowns between Scotland and England, in 1603, many French words were used in Scottish kitchens. My recipe is based on one from Elizabeth Cleland's *A New and Easy Method of Cookery*, written in 1755. There were still then, and are even now, culinary terms derived from the French. We still call a leg of lamb a *gigot*; we still call a large platter an ashet, from *assiette*.

According to F. Marian McNeill, sauty bannocks were made on Shrove Tuesday and traditionally consisted of oatmeal, eggs, beef 'bree' (broth) or milk, and were cooked on a hot girdle rubbed with fat. She writes, 'The making of the bannocks was a great ploy, in which all present participated.'

The original recipe for these delicious oatmeal pancakes called for 'a chopin of milk' to be boiled and a 'mutchkin of oatmeal' to be stirred in first. The flavourings (lemon and nutmeg) are what Mrs Cleland stipulated. They are light yet have a good, nutty texture from the oatmeal. An ideal breakfast pancake.

Mrs Cleland's suggestion was to 'serve hot with beat butter, orange, and sugar'. I have given the recipe for fairy butter on the following page for an even more delightfully eighteenth-century treat.

Bring the milk to the boil, then gradually stir in the oatmeal, a little at a time. Once it is all added, remove from the heat. Now, get in with a balloon whisk and beat madly to ensure there are no lumps. Allow to cool, then beat in the remaining ingredients.

Heat a girdle (or heavy-based frying pan) to medium-hot and lightly wipe with butter. Once hot, drop dessertspoonfuls of the mixture onto the surface and cook as for Scotch pancakes: 2–3 minutes one side, then, once large bubbles appear, flip over and continue to cook the other side.

After 1–2 minutes, remove and keep warm by covering with a tea towel.

Serve with a smear of butter for breakfast, or with a dollop of fairy butter for pudding.

Fairy butter

I developed this from Elizabeth Cleland's recipe, featured in her 1755 cookery book. She advocates serving this as it is, in little heaps on plates, which must have been a fairly rich dessert, perhaps served with dainty biscuits and a glass of sweet wine. F. Marian McNeill (whose source is Mrs Dalgairns's recipe from 1829) suggests soaking some Naples biscuits in white wine, then putting over them some fairy butter 'in heaps as high as it can be raised'.

Mrs MacIver also includes a recipe for fairy butter in her 1773 book. As well as another hard-boiled egg yolk, she suggests adding orange flower water or rose water. To serve, she elaborates on how to make the 'heaps'. She writes: 'put it into a squirt, and squirt it on an ashet in little heaps'. According to Lara Haggerty, the Keeper of Books at the wonderful Innerpeffray Library, a 'squirt' was a form of piping bag in the eighteenth century. Ever since I read those words, I feel obliged to call my piping bag a squirt – far more satisfactory.

I like this as a floral-tasting butter icing for chocolate cakes, or to serve with Christmas pudding instead of brandy butter – or dolloped onto hot pancakes, such as the sauty bannocks.

Makes 1 small bowlful

•

yolks of 2 hard-boiled eggs

100g butter, softened

150g icing sugar, sifted

1 tbsp orange flower water
(or rose water)

Beat the yolks and butter together. Once well amalgamated, sift in the icing sugar and add the flower water, then beat until smooth.

Fatty cutties

This recipe comes from Orkney, and on each of its many islands there are variations. Some have more butter, some more dried fruit; some have a little beremeal as well as plain flour.

The fatty cuttie originated many years ago when people were very poor and daily bread took the form of a girdle bannock, usually made from beremeal. As people became slightly better off, they began to use plain wheat flour instead of barley and also started to add fat (butter) to their breads and cakes. Eventually these fat-enriched cakes came to be known as fatty cutties because they contained some fat and because they were cut into wedges, quarters or rectangles before baking.

During my last visit to Westray, I managed to try some of Rita Stout's fatty cutties. These are thinner than most and are rectangles, about 10cm long and 5cm wide. Another Westray baker, Netta Harcus, makes hers slightly thicker. Both are delicious. Netta and Rita use the same recipe of 3 cups of plain flour, 1 block of butter, 1 cup of sugar, a quarter teaspoon of baking soda and half a cup of currants. The ratio in my recipe uses a little less butter, but do add an extra 25g for even more richness if you like.

Makes 8

•

175g plain flour

¼ tsp bicarbonate of soda

75g caster sugar

75g currants

75g butter, melted

1 tbsp (approx.) milk

butter, to cook

Mix the flour and bicarbonate of soda in a bowl. Stir in the sugar and currants. Melt the butter and add to the flour with just enough milk to combine to a stiff dough. You may need to add another half tablespoon or so. Knead very lightly and divide into two balls.

Roll each ball into a round shape, about 5mm thick, then cut into four wedges or rectangles. Preheat your girdle or heavy frying pan to medium-hot, butter very lightly, then cook the fatty cutties for 3 – 4 minutes on each side until golden brown. Serve warm without butter, or cold with a thin smear of butter.

Like scones, these are always best eaten on the day they are made.

Sour scones

Makes 6

•

200g self-raising flour

25g medium oatmeal

½ tsp baking powder

½ tsp caraway seeds

2 tsp caster sugar

175ml (approx.) sour milk

This is a variation from a recipe in F. Marian McNeill's *The Scots Kitchen*. She says the recipe for 'Sour-Skons' is from Orkney and that you must first soak some oatmeal in buttermilk for a few days. Presumably the result would be a rather sour-tasting scone. There are also caraway seeds and a little sugar in her recipe.

I like to use sour milk, just like my mum used to bake her scones with – it gives a lovely light texture – though nowadays it takes a long time for milk to smell sour. Otherwise, use 150ml of buttermilk and a splash or two of regular milk to give you the correct consistency. Or you can use a 150ml tub of soured cream, again adding a few splashes of regular milk to bind.

These scones would traditionally have been baked on the girdle.

For those of you used to making scones with butter (and egg), don't worry – there is no misprint. This traditional recipe has neither, but it does not take anything away from the finished scone.

Eat these warm with lashings of butter and jam – and a cup of tea. Or leave out the sugar in the recipe and spread with a thick layer of butter and a sliver of farmhouse cheese and eat with a bowl of soup.

Butter a baking sheet. Preheat the oven to 220°C.

Place the flour, oatmeal, baking powder, caraway seeds and sugar in a bowl and stir together. Make a well in the middle and add the sour milk – enough to combine to a softish dough. Using floured hands, pat out on a floured board and cut into six scones, then bake for about 15 minutes or until well risen. Remove to a wire rack and eat warm.

Beremeal bannocks

This is my adaptation of Paul Doull's recipe from The Foveran, his restaurant and hotel near Kirkwall, on Orkney. Bere is an ancient barley that has grown on the islands for many centuries and is still milled at Barony Mill, an old watermill in Birsay, then ground into beremeal. It has a strong, earthy taste, so I like to make these bannocks with half wheat flour, half beremeal to lighten the flavour.

An old Shetland recipe I have for these stipulates adding bicarbonate of soda to counteract the acids found in beremeal, hence its inclusion here, along with the self-raising flour and cream of tartar.

These Orcadian specialities are delicious served with butter and soused herring, smoked salmon pâté or a farmhouse cheese.

Makes 2 bannocks

•

butter, to cook

75g beremeal

75g self-raising flour

1 tsp bicarbonate of soda

1 rounded tsp cream of tartar

¼ tsp salt

100ml buttermilk

75 – 100ml cold water

First put the girdle or solid frying pan on till it reaches a steady heat: this can take at least 5 minutes. Very lightly butter the surface.

Mix the flours, bicarbonate of soda, cream of tartar and salt in a bowl. Make a well in the middle and add the buttermilk, then enough cold water to combine to a soft dough.

Tip onto a board dusted with a little beremeal and shape gently into two bannock shapes: rounds about 12cm in diameter and about 2.5cm thick. (They puff up as they cook.) Use a very light touch and do not knead.

Slap them onto the girdle and cook, without touching, for 5 minutes, then turn and continue to cook for 4 minutes until cooked through. Both top and bottom will be scorched all over with a golden brown.

Remove and place on a wire rack and loosely cover with a tea towel to keep the top soft. Tempting though it is to devour them hot, leave it until they are barely warm or cold before splitting open and spreading with a little butter.

Oatcakes

Makes 8

•

150g medium oatmeal

25g pinhead oatmeal

25g porridge oats

½ tsp salt

½ tsp baking powder

50g butter

50ml boiling water

Although oatcakes are traditionally made on the girdle, I have given an oven method below, since most cooks are more familiar with baking trays than girdles. The girdle method is also given; the classic way is to cook one side on the girdle, then toast them on a special toasting stone in front of the fire. A brief spell in a low oven will also finish them off. The reason they are not turned over on the girdle to finish the cooking is that this would make them tough.

Once cool, oatcakes are traditionally stored in a 'girnel' (oatmeal chest) to keep crisp. I bury mine in a large Tupperware box I keep porridge oats in.

The finished texture will depend on the type of oatmeal you use. I like to use a base of medium and either pinhead or fine, for a rough or smooth texture. There are also regional variations on the thickness of the oatcake, from thin and crispy to thick and rough.

In the following recipe, depending on how rough or fine you want the texture to be, you can use all oatmeal (200g) and leave out the pinhead and porridge oats, but the combination here does give a good coarse bite without being too crunchy.

Butter a baking tray. Preheat the oven to 170°C.

Place the first five ingredients in a bowl and stir. Melt the butter in 50ml of boiling water, then combine this with the oats and mix briefly to form a fairly stiff dough.

Sprinkle some oatmeal (fine or medium) over a board and gently roll out the mixture thinly to a circle, about 23cm in diameter. Cut into eight wedges and transfer these carefully to the buttered oven tray. Bake for about 20 minutes until just firm. Remove carefully to a wire rack to cool.

GIRDLE METHOD

Preheat the oven to 140°C.

Bake the oatcakes, four at a time, on a lightly buttered girdle over a moderate heat for 4–5 minutes on one side only. Once they are light brown underneath, transfer to a wire rack. Place this on a baking tray and set in the oven for about 25 minutes or until they have completely dried out.

Cheesy oatcakes

These crispy oatcakes are good served with a smear of butter or soft goat's cheese. They are also wonderful with a sliver of blue cheese and a spoonful of crunchy honeycomb.

Butter a baking tray. Preheat the oven to 170°C.

Place the oats, oatmeal, flour, cheese and salt in a bowl. Melt the butter in 100ml of hot water, then slowly add this to the mixture in the bowl and combine into a ball with your hands. Do not overwork.

Roll out gently on a lightly floured board and cut into rounds with a biscuit cutter.

Transfer to the buttered baking tray and bake for about 30 minutes, or until they have crisped up and are cooked through. Transfer to a wire rack to cool.

Makes 18–20

•

25g porridge oats

125g medium oatmeal

50g self-raising flour

50g mature cheddar cheese, finely grated

½ tsp salt

25g butter

100ml hot water

Seeded oatcakes

Makes 24–28

•

175g medium oatmeal,
plus extra

100g wholemeal self-raising
flour

1 tbsp poppy seeds

1 tbsp sunflower seeds

a grinding of black pepper

½ tsp salt

75g butter

150ml hot water

These are a doddle to make and are also very versatile. They are less fragile than traditional ones made from oats only. Instead of the seeds I've listed, you could add golden linseed or sesame seeds, or alternatively a tablespoon of freshly chopped thyme leaves.

Serve smeared with butter and with a slice of cheese.

Butter a baking sheet. Preheat the oven to 150°C.

Mix the oatmeal and flour, then add the seeds, the black pepper and salt. Melt the butter in 150ml of hot water, then pour this into the bowl, stirring gently with a metal spoon until combined – you might not need all the liquid.

Sprinkle a large board generously with oatmeal and tip out the mixture, combining into a ball with hands dabbed in oatmeal. Roll out thinly, then cut into rounds, using a fluted or plain cutter.

Place on the baking sheet and bake for about 45 minutes or until cooked through and crisp. Cool on a wire rack.

4
Brownies, traybakes & muffins

Chocolate brownies (and Raspberry brownies)

Salted caramel brownies

Toffee oat bars

Fudgey coconut chocolate bars

Sticky walnut shortbread squares

Chocolate, cherry and coconut traybake

Chocolate tiffin with honeycomb

Roasted rhubarb, orange and ginger blondies

Nanaimo bars

Date and ginger crumble shortbread

Marshmallow millionaire shortbread

Dairy-free and egg-free raspberry muffins

Wheat-free raisin muffins

Poppy seed and lemon muffins

Crowdie, feta and black olive muffins

Introduction

The term 'traybake' is relatively new in the lexicon of Scottish baking. 'Teabreads' was generally recognised as the word covering all manner of cakes/scones/biscuits – and also anything baked in a tin and cut into squares. There were regional variations: in Aberdeenshire, a cup of tea – 'a fly cup' – was usually accompanied by a 'fine piece', which was something tasty, sweet and invariably home-baked.

But the word traybake, to my knowledge, has only come to being in Scotland in the past few decades, though admittedly we had millionaire's shortbread and tiffin, but I certainly never heard the term during my 1960s childhood.

Perhaps it was the arrival of the 'brownie' that made us think how almost exotic the term traybake sounded. The brownie, of course, came with attendant woes: it was often too dry, as we were so used to testing cakes with a cocktail stick (which had to come out clean) that they were frequently overbaked. They were also often just not chocolatey enough: Scotbloc was the 'chocolate' used in most bakes, as there was simply no such thing as good quality cooking chocolate for most home bakers. Thankfully, things have moved on and brownies, and indeed traybakes, are made with top quality ingredients: butter always lending a far better flavour than the blocks of margarine of old.

Muffins have been with us for a long time – but invariably they were the English-style muffins, the type sold in Drury Lane and which now sit happily under poached eggs and hollandaise sauce in eggs benedict. But, now, sweet muffins abound and are not dissimilar to what we used to call 'buns' or fairy cakes. And as for the divine savoury muffins I first encountered some 20 years ago in New Zealand . . . Once tasted, never forgotten.

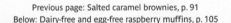

Previous page: Salted caramel brownies, p. 91
Below: Dairy-free and egg-free raspberry muffins, p. 105

Chocolate brownies
(and Raspberry brownies)

Who doesn't love a brownie? They are versatile and delicious, with their characteristic squidgy, fudgey, moist middle and thin layer of crispy crust on top. As well as serving up these delectable squares of joy with tea or coffee, brownies are wonderful served with a glass of ice-cold milk. You can also serve this whole, as a brownie cake: instead of cutting it into squares, leave it until it's completely cold before decanting it whole, ready to ice with ganache or rich chocolate butter icing. Another idea is to serve tiny squares of brownie as petits fours.

They are also perfect for pudding, warmed slightly and served with a dollop of best ice cream and some fruit, such as berries, sliced mango or pineapple, or poached pear slices. Pour a slug of crème de cassis or Cointreau over the lot and you have a truly memorable pudding.

For a change to your regular brownies, you can add 100g of chopped walnuts, pecans or dried apricots to the batter and bake as normal.

In the summer, when the raspberries are plentiful in gardens and pick-your-own farms, make raspberry brownies. Since the berries are delicate, do not add them as you would the nuts or apricots. Rather, tip just over half of the brownie mixture into the tin, then scatter over about 175g of fresh raspberries and cover with the remaining mixture. Raspberry brownies are delicious, the tartness of the berries balancing the richness of the brownie so well, and I love them.

Whenever I make respberry brownies, I'm taken back to the north-east of Scotland some 25 years ago. I was doing a baking demonstration in Sutherland, and as I finished spreading the thick gloop of luscious raw brownie batter over the raspberries, I looked up at my audience of local Highland ladies and noticed a hand shoot up. A question about how much baking powder I had added to the batter? Were frozen berries suitable to use in the winter? No, the question from this respectable-looking middle-aged lady in a kilt was unexpected.

'Sue,' she said, 'do you ever put cannabis in your brownies?'

Not usually lost for words, I momentarily faltered, but then, all too aware there was a journalist in my audience, decided to deflect rather than challenge. I therefore cross-referred to a recipe for haschich fudge from a fascinating book sitting on my shelves at home – *The Alice B. Toklas Cookbook*, written about her time living in Paris with Gertrude Stein – all the while trying to concentrate on my own, totally licit, brownies.

Afterwards, as we chatted over tea and scones, I spotted the be-kilted questioner and asked her if she spoke from experience. She chuckled and said she couldn't possibly comment, but she had recently had a visit from the local police asking if they could check out the tomato plants in her greenhouse . . .

Makes 16–20

•

200g butter

200g best quality dark
chocolate

250g dark muscovado sugar

3 eggs

1 tsp vanilla extract

100g plain flour

1 tsp baking powder

pinch of salt

175g raspberries (optional)

Preheat the oven to 190°C.

Lightly butter and base-line a 23cm square brownie tin with baking parchment.

Place the butter and chocolate in a heatproof bowl over a pan of simmering water – or in the microwave – and stir until melted.

Beat together the sugar, eggs and vanilla until frothy, ensuring any lumps in the sugar are eliminated.

Beat the buttery chocolate into the sugar mixture, then add in the flour and baking powder with a pinch of salt. (Add nuts or apricots here, if using). Fold everything together gently.

Tip into the prepared tin. (If using raspberries, layer half the batter, scatter over the berries, then top with the remaining batter.)

Bake in the preheated oven for 18–20 minutes (no more) until a crust has formed. For the raspberry brownies, you may need a couple of minutes longer.

Remove and cool for a couple of hours until completely cold before cutting.

Salted caramel brownies

The fad of salted caramel refuses to go away, so why not just give in to it? Here are some exquisite brownies that have not only caramel inside, but also a welcome tang from a little salt.

The main thing to remember when making these brownies is to remove them from the oven when they are just set and a crust has formed; any longer and they could either burn or overcook. Leave for a couple of hours or overnight before cutting.

Though I suggest this makes 20 brownies, you can also cut them into tiny squares so they are almost bite size – the perfect sweet canapé.

These are the most requested brownies in my family. And once you bite through the deeply chocolatey exterior to the soft salty caramel, you will hopefully see why.

Preheat the oven to 190°C.

Lightly butter and base-line a 23cm square brownie tin with baking parchment.

Place the butter and chocolate in a heatproof bowl over a pan of simmering water – or in the microwave – and stir until melted.

Beat together the sugar and eggs, ensuring there are no lumps in the sugar. Beat the buttery chocolate into the sugar mixture, then add in the flour and baking powder.

Tip about two-thirds of the mixture into the prepared pan. Using two teaspoons, dot blobs of caramel all over, then evenly scatter the sea salt. Top with the remaining mixture, spreading carefully – it is thick, but try to ensure all the caramel is covered.

Bake for about 18 minutes, or until a crust has formed. It will still feel a little wobbly underneath. Remove and cool for a couple of hours, then refrigerate for at least 2 hours (or overnight) before cutting.

Makes 20

•

200g butter

200g best quality dark chocolate

225g dark muscovado sugar

3 eggs

100g plain flour

1 tsp baking powder

½ a 397g tin of Nestlé caramel – use the other half for the Chocolate caramel wafers on p. 251

1 tsp sea salt

Toffee oat bars

Makes 24

•

125g porridge oats

200g plain flour

150g light muscovado sugar

½ tsp bicarbonate of soda

pinch of salt

150g butter, diced

150ml whole milk

200g plain toffees

These are decadent in the extreme and yet, with the addition of oats, not entirely unhealthy! I usually use regular plain toffee for this recipe, but treacle toffee makes a nice change.

Preheat the oven to 180°C.

Butter a swiss-roll tin (23 × 33cm).

Place the oats, flour, sugar and bicarbonate of soda in a food processor with a pinch of salt. Process briefly then add the butter and process briefly again until the mixture starts to come together.

Press about three-quarters of this into the tin, spreading out with (floured) hands to form an even base.

Place the milk and toffees together in a saucepan over a low heat, stirring until smooth and melted. This takes about 10 minutes.

Pour this slowly over the base, leaving a tiny margin around the edges, then sprinkle the remaining oat mixture like a crumble topping.

Bake in the oven for about 20 minutes or until the edges are golden brown. Cut around the edges to loosen, then leave on a wire rack to cool completely before cutting into small squares.

Fudgey coconut chocolate bars

This divine recipe is adapted from Anta Pottery's 'Magic Bars', which I discovered in Anta's café near Tain in Ross-shire. The taste is coconutty, fudgey and chocolatey.

Like most traybakes, these freeze well. So you can make a batch, and, when it has cooled and you have 'tested' your bake, place the other bars in bags and freeze until you have guests popping in for coffee – or you feel the need to have one yourself. They defrost very quickly.

———————

Preheat the oven to 180°C.

Lightly butter a swiss-roll tin (23 × 33cm).

Mix the butter and biscuits together, then spread into the tin, pressing down firmly to level.

Slowly pour over the tin of condensed milk, leaving a tiny margin around the edges so it does not stick to the sides.

Scatter over the chocolate, distributing it evenly.

Finally top with the coconut. Pat it down firmly with the palms of your hands to ensure it is compact.

Bake for about 20 minutes until golden brown, covering loosely with foil after 10 minutes or so, if the coconut is becoming too brown.

Loosen the edges with a knife, then allow to cool completely before cutting into bars.

Makes 24

•

150g butter, melted

400g digestive biscuits, crumbed

1 tin (397g) condensed milk

250g best quality milk chocolate, chopped into tiny chunks (or coarsely grated)

150g desiccated coconut

Sticky walnut shortbread squares

Makes 20

·

For the shortbread base

125g butter (hard from the fridge), diced

175g plain flour

40g demerara sugar

·

For the topping

75g desiccated coconut

100g walnuts, roughly chopped

150g dark muscovado sugar

2 eggs

½ tsp baking powder

1 tsp ground cinnamon

I always taste such wonderful things during my many visits to Shetland. On a recent trip, I had some delicious home baking at my friend Isabel Johnson's house in Lerwick. The following recipe is based on hers, which in turn was based on an ancient cutting from a newspaper. Warning: one is never enough!

———————

Preheat the oven to 180°C.

Butter a square 20cm cake tin.

For the base, place everything in a food processor and whizz until it resembles breadcrumbs. Tip this into the baking tin and press down firmly all over to make a level base. Bake for 15 minutes, then remove.

For the topping, place everything in the food processor (I don't bother to wash it in between) and whizz everything together until delightfully sticky.

Carefully spread this over the base, levelling it out with a palette knife.

Bake for a further 15 minutes until firm.

Remove and allow to cool in the tin, cutting into squares after an hour or so. Remove from the tin once completely cold

Chocolate, cherry
and coconut traybake

Makes 24 pieces

•

450g best quality chocolate
(I like ⅔ milk, ⅓ dark)

200g glacé cherries

4 medium eggs

175g caster sugar

250g desiccated coconut

This recipe was part of my childhood. Though my mum did not make it, I used to enjoy it at various friends' houses and I have always loved it. There is something about the moist coconut studded with scarlet cherries on top of a thick chocolate base that is so moreish.

It is a doddle to make, but you must leave the tray in the fridge for the specified time, so the chocolate can fully set after it has been baked. If you try to lever out the pieces while the chocolate is still soft, it will simply all collapse. I recommend going out for a long walk as it cools and sets – the inviting aromas are just too tempting.

Butter a swiss-roll tin (23 × 33cm).

Melt the chocolate (I usually do it in a microwave but you can also do it on the stove, using a glass bowl sitting within a pan of very gently simmering water), then pour it into the base of the prepared tin.

Smooth out with the back of a spoon. Allow to cool and harden completely.

Preheat the oven to 180°C.

Halve the cherries and place at intervals over the chocolate.

Beat the eggs in a bowl, then add the sugar and coconut. Stir until well combined, then carefully spoon this mixture over the cherries, taking care not to push the cherries into one corner. Pat down gently to smooth the surface.

Bake for about 25 minutes until the coconut mixture looks golden brown and feels firm to the touch.

Leave to cool for at least 30 minutes before marking into squares, then allow to become completely cold. Place in the fridge for another 30 minutes or so until completely hard before removing the squares from the tin.

Chocolate tiffin
with honeycomb

There are many variations of tiffin, and indeed sometimes I add a couple of tablespoons of raisins, chopped hazelnuts and desiccated coconut instead of the Crunchie bars.

Also, it's not essential to cover it with chocolate, but I think the overall effect is neater and more alluring.

It is important not to crush the biscuits too finely, as you would, say, for a cheesecake base. You want good chunks throughout. Similarly, you want nuggets of honeycomb, not smashed-up crumbs.

As in all recipes using chocolate, only best quality will do, otherwise it will taste sickly.

Lightly butter a 23cm square cake tin and lay two long pieces of baking parchment inside (one at right angles to the other), so that they have overhanging edges; this helps ease out the whole tiffin.

Melt the butter, syrup and chocolate in a bowl in a microwave (or on the stove in a glass bowl sitting within a pan of very gently simmering water).

Place the biscuits in a large plastic bag and bash with a rolling pin, ensuring they are not too well crushed: you want mainly crumbs to mix well into the melted chocolate – but also lots of chunks for texture too. (You can also do this in a food processor using the Pulse button, but you tend to get fewer chunks this way.)

Do the same with the Crunchies, bashing them up into crumbs and chunks.

Once the chocolate mixture has melted, add the biscuits and Crunchies, combine thoroughly, then tip into the tin, pressing down with the back of a spoon to level it out.

Melt the chocolate for the topping, then pour this over the base. When cool, chill well in the fridge and cut into squares once solid and set.

Makes 20 squares

•

200g butter

2 tbsp golden syrup

200g best quality
dark chocolate

100g best quality
milk chocolate

300g rich tea biscuits

8 regular size (26g)
Crunchie bars

•

For the topping

150g best quality chocolate
(half milk, half plain)

Roasted rhubarb, orange and ginger blondies

Try to find early season, pink rhubarb for these delectable blondies. They will still taste good if it's later in the season and the stems of rhubarb are greener, but you won't get the visual 'wow' factor – the glorious pink contrasting against the brown of the blondie mixture.

For the rhubarb, preheat the oven to 200°C.

Place the rhubarb in a roasting tray, taking care each piece is separate, if possible. Sprinkle over the sugar, then the zest. Leave for 10 minutes or so, then place in the oven, uncovered, for about 10 minutes or until the syrup is bubbling and the rhubarb is tender.

For the blondies, reduce the oven to 180°C.

Butter a 20cm square cake tin and line with baking parchment, letting some overhang the sides (This helps you to remove the blondies from the tin.)

Melt the butter until just molten (not completely liquid: I do this in the microwave for a couple of turns), then add the two sugars and mix until smooth. Beat in the egg, then gently stir in the flour, the salt, and the ground and stem ginger. Tip this mixture into the prepared tin, smoothing the top. Press in the pieces of rhubarb all over (try to envisage how you will cut it into squares and work on 2–3 pieces of rhubarb per square).

Place in the oven for about 25 minutes or until set. Remove and allow to cool for about 20 minutes or so before lifting out the whole bake using the baking parchment. Place on a chopping board to cool completely, then cut into squares.

Makes 16

•

300g (approx.) rhubarb, trimmed, chopped into 2cm pieces

60g demerara sugar

grated zest of ½ an orange

•

For the blondies

125g butter

100g light muscovado sugar

75g demerara sugar

1 egg

125g self-raising flour

½ tsp salt

2 tsp ground ginger

2 tbsp stem ginger (approx. 3 balls from a jar), diced

Nanaimo bars

Makes 24

•

For the base

110g butter

50g caster sugar

40g cocoa powder

1 egg, beaten

225g digestives, crushed

100g desiccated coconut

•

For the filling

110g butter, softened

3 tbsp custard powder
(I use Bird's)

250g icing sugar

2 tbsp whole milk

1 tsp vanilla extract

•

For the topping

225g best quality
dark chocolate

50g butter

I have made Nanaimo bars for a while and was pretty happy with my results, but when I tasted Edinburgh-based baker Tara Heron's I knew I had to fiddle with my original recipe, as hers is sublime.

In an ancient Canadian recipe book I have, it states that the origin of the word 'Nanaimo' is a city of that name on Vancouver Island. That recipe has no custard powder in it and a combination of walnuts and coconut in the base. Other recipes have almonds and coconut. But the thing that, to me, makes them look so gorgeous is the pale yellow filling, so a touch of custard powder is required.

Tara was brought up in Brandon, in Manitoba, Canada, and she says that these bars were very much a part of her childhood. She remembers being taken along as a kid to visit family, and when she was offered a small selection of 'dainties', and saw Nanaimo bars on the tray, she realised the visit was, in fact, worthwhile.

Here is my version, based on Tara's and my traditional recipe. She recommends making them in individual moulds (you can buy silicone ones), as then they will look pretty perfect. If you make them in one big slab, it can be difficult to cut the chocolate without it cracking a little . . . but if you dip the knife in very hot water before cutting, your bars will still look pretty good. And they will taste divine.

———————

Lightly butter a square 23cm cake tin, or if making individual bars lightly oil 16 silicone moulds with a base of 5cm square.

For the base, melt the butter, sugar and cocoa together in a pan over a very low heat. Beat in the egg and stir well until smooth, then remove from the heat and stir in the biscuits and coconut.

Tip into the square cake tin (or divide between the moulds), pressing down to level out. Chill for an hour or so.

For the filling, beat the butter well. Sift the custard powder and icing sugar together, then add to the bowl and beat well. Ideally, do this with electric beaters or in a food mixer with the whisk attachment. Once combined and smooth, add the milk and vanilla, and continue to beat until creamy. Spread this over the base (or bases) and smooth out carefully. Chill again for another hour or so.

For the topping, melt the chocolate and butter together (I do this in the microwave) and pour over the filling (or divide between the moulds). Tap the tin or moulds on your worktop to smooth it and remove any air bubbles, then chill till fully set – this will take at least a couple of hours, or even overnight.

If making individual bars, pop out each mould. If using a whole tin, dip a knife into very hot water, then cut slices as quickly as possible, wiping it clean on kitchen paper as you go. They are best kept in the fridge – just remove them about half an hour before serving.

Date and ginger
crumble shortbread

Makes 16

•

200g dried dates,
stoned and chopped

25g butter

grated zest of 1 orange

3 tbsp orange juice

2 balls stem ginger, diced

2 tbsp syrup from the
stem ginger jar

•

For the shortbread

200g butter, slightly softened

100g caster sugar

250g plain flour

50g semolina

pinch of salt

1 tsp demerara sugar

These little squares are delicious with a cup of tea – or are perfect to take on picnics.

Be sure to leave them till they are completely cold in the tin or they will collapse.

Place the first six ingredients in a pan and bring to the boil, then lower the heat and simmer, covered, for about 5 minutes or until the dates are soft. Remove from the heat, tip into a small food processor and whizz. Leave to cool.

Preheat the oven to 170°C and butter a square 23cm tin.

For the shortbread, beat the butter and caster sugar together until light and fluffy – it will take about 10 minutes – then gradually add the flour and semolina, along with a pinch of salt. Combine very briefly, until it just comes together as a dough.

Tip two-thirds of this mixture into the buttered tin, pressing down. Spread out the cooled date mixture on top, then break up the remaining shortbread into little nuggets and sprinkle all over the dates. Press down lightly with the palms of your hands, then bake for 30–40 minutes until golden. Remove to a wire rack and sprinkle with the demerara sugar.

Cut into squares while hot, then leave until completely cold before removing from the tin.

Marshmallow millionaire shortbread

This recipe is from Nicola Fitz-Hardy, who runs the hugely popular Craigard Kitchen on Islay. It is one of her most popular bakes.

––––––––

Preheat the oven to 160°C.

Line a swiss-roll tin (23 × 33cm) with baking parchment.

For the shortbread, place the butter and sugar in your food mixer and beat together well. Add the flour and mix until it looks like breadcrumbs. Tip the mixture into your lined baking tray and press down with the back of a spoon to make an even layer. Prick all over with a fork.

Bake on the middle shelf of the oven for about 25 minutes or until light golden brown, then cool.

While the base is cooling, prepare your marshmallow layer. Cover the shortbread with rows of marshmallows, alternating pink with white if using. Any gaps will be filled with caramel.

For the caramel, put the butter, sugar, syrup and condensed milk in a heavy-based pan on a low heat to melt. Stir regularly to ensure it does not catch on the bottom of the pan. Once the ingredients have melted and there are no lumps, turn up the heat to medium. Keep stirring until the mixture comes to the boil. Continue to stir for at least 5 minutes – you will have big bubbles. Just keep stirring!

Pour the caramel gently over the marshmallow-covered base, trying to fill any gaps. The marshmallows will slightly melt into the caramel – it will all settle and flatten out.

Leave to cool.

In the microwave, melt your chocolate for the topping, then, when melted, pour it over the cooled caramel/marshmallow mixture, spreading to smooth it out. Finish off with a handful of mini marshmallows. Cover with baking parchment and cool in the fridge for at least an hour until the chocolate is set, then cut into pieces.

Makes 24

•

For the shortbread

250g cold butter, chopped into chunks

125g caster sugar

340g plain flour

•

For the marshmallow layer

500g × standard size marshmallows

•

For the caramel

200g butter

3 tbsp caster sugar

4 tbsp golden syrup

1 × tin (397g) condensed milk

•

For the chocolate layer

200g best quality milk chocolate

handful of mini marshmallows

Dairy-free and egg-free raspberry muffins

These are moist and packed with flavour. Designed for my youngest grandson, Oliver, who has had a dairy and egg allergy, they are also favourites of the other little ones, with the burst of raspberry and hint of spice. They are best eaten slightly warm.

You can substitute blueberries or brambles for the raspberries.

Place 12 paper cases (regular size, not American/large size) in a 12-hole bun tin. Preheat the oven to 200°C.

Place the oil and vinegar in a bowl and add 150ml of cold water. Stir, then add the sugar, flour, oats, baking powder and cinnamon. Combine gently, then carefully fold in the raspberries, taking care not to break them up.

Fill the muffin cases with the mixture, then bake for about 20–25 minutes until well risen and golden brown.

Makes 12

•

100ml sunflower oil

1 tbsp white wine or cider vinegar

150ml cold water

150g caster sugar

150g plain flour

50g porridge oats

1 rounded tsp baking powder

¼ tsp ground cinnamon

200g raspberries

Wheat-free raisin muffins

Makes 12

•

150g rice flour (ground rice)

70g medium oatmeal

1½ tsp baking powder

½ tsp bicarbonate of soda

50g desiccated coconut

70g light muscovado sugar

100g raisins

grated zest of 1 lemon

2 tbsp lemon juice
(approx. juice of 1 lemon)

75ml sunflower oil

100ml milk

1 egg

These are ideal for anyone intolerant to wheat, as they contain only rice flour, oatmeal and coconut. They are so utterly delicious – light, crumbly, almost crunchy – that I highly recommend them for everyone.

Warm, just out of the oven, they make the most wonderful breakfast treat.

Place 12 paper bun/muffin cases in a bun tray. Preheat the oven to 190°C.

Combine the first eight ingredients in a bowl.

Mix the next four ingredients in a jug, then pour into the bowl, stirring gently.

Stir very briefly to mix, then, once combined, fill the cases in the bun tray.

Bake for 20 minutes until risen and golden.

Poppy seed and lemon muffins

The combination of lemon and poppy seeds is excellent and one that I first came across in Sydney in the shape of dainty little friands – buttery two-bite-size cakes.

I have adapted the recipe so that it can be made into either large muffins, ideal for breakfast or brunch, or dainty friands that are ideal with afternoon tea.

Place eight large paper muffin cases in a bun tin or butter 14–16 mini muffin or friand moulds. Preheat the oven to 190°C.

Place the first three ingredients in a bowl, then stir in the lemon zest. Make a well in the centre, then tip in the oil, eggs and lemon juice. Stir gently until combined, then spoon into the paper cases or buttered moulds.

Bake in the preheated oven for 15–20 minutes for the friands, and 25 minutes for the muffins.

Makes 8 American-style muffins (or 14–16 friands)

•

150g caster sugar

150g self-raising flour

25g poppy seeds

grated zest and juice of 1 medium lemon

125ml sunflower oil

2 eggs

Crowdie, feta and black olive muffins

Makes 12

•

250g plain flour

2 tsp baking powder

½ tsp bicarbonate of soda

freshly ground black pepper

1 egg

200ml milk

125g butter, melted and cooled a little

3 rounded tbsp crowdie (or cottage cheese)

150g feta, patted dry and chopped

100g black olives, pitted and chopped

Crowdie is a traditional Scottish cheese, not dissimilar to cottage cheese, made by crofters. Hand-skimmed on crofts, it was a universal breakfast dish all over Scotland. Indeed, according to F. Marian McNeill, 'Crowdie-time' is an old name for breakfast time, used in both poetry (Burns) and literature (Sir Walter Scott).

Catherine Brown, in her *Scottish Cookery*, has a recipe for 'Cream-Crowdie' (cranachan). In this, two parts crowdie are mixed with one part whipped cream and these are mixed, according to taste, with toasted oatmeal, seasonal berries, heather honey and whisky. This was usually eaten to celebrate the end of harvest time.

These muffins are no less delicious, though more suitable for brunch than an autumnal feast. I first discovered savoury muffins in New Zealand many years before they were a regular café item in this country. This recipe is for a light, tangy muffin that also looks wonderful, with the addition of the black olives studded throughout.

You can use cottage cheese, if you can't find any crowdie.

These are best eaten warm soon after they emerge from the oven. If you are not eating them the same day, freeze them in freezer bags, then reheat in a medium oven until thoroughly defrosted and warmed through.

———

Put 12 muffin cases in a bun tray. Preheat the oven to 190°C.

Add the first three ingredients to a bowl with a grinding of fresh black pepper.

In another bowl, whisk the egg, milk and melted cooled butter.

Gently stir the crowdie, feta and olives into the flour, along with the liquid, folding everything together as gently as possible, but making sure it is all combined. Do not overmix or they will be tough.

Spoon the mixture into the 12 muffin cases and bake for 20–22 minutes until well-risen and golden. Eat warm.

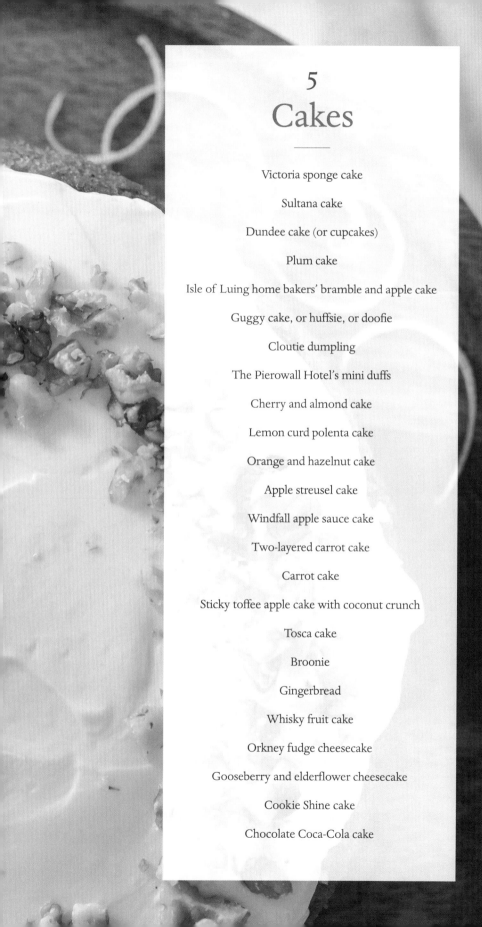

5
Cakes

Victoria sponge cake

Sultana cake

Dundee cake (or cupcakes)

Plum cake

Isle of Luing home bakers' bramble and apple cake

Guggy cake, or huffsie, or doofie

Cloutie dumpling

The Pierowall Hotel's mini duffs

Cherry and almond cake

Lemon curd polenta cake

Orange and hazelnut cake

Apple streusel cake

Windfall apple sauce cake

Two-layered carrot cake

Carrot cake

Sticky toffee apple cake with coconut crunch

Tosca cake

Broonie

Gingerbread

Whisky fruit cake

Orkney fudge cheesecake

Gooseberry and elderflower cheesecake

Cookie Shine cake

Chocolate Coca-Cola cake

Introduction

Who doesn't love a cake? As a child, it meant celebration – a birthday or some other special occasion that required a whole cake as opposed to the various slices and slabs inside the cake tins stacked in the larder. Nowadays, though, there are cakes in cafés, cakes in kitchens when you visit – and a great deal of cakes on television! Probably programmes such as *The Great British Bake Off* have done most to demote the cake (in the best possible sense) from 'special treat only' to more and more commonplace.

All over Scotland, there are regional variations of cake – for example, Orkney broonie or Shetland huffsie; this chapter also deals with the contemporary and international, the ones you are likely to find in a hipster café, a gorgeous French pâtisserie or Italian pasticceria.

The main thing about cake, to me, is that it is for sharing. As the baker cuts slices for those around the table or at a picnic, or wherever, there is a sense of taking and receiving; there's a connection as everyone shares. No other bake – or indeed dish – has this capacity to bring everyone together over one thing: a delicious, home-baked cake.

Previous page: Two-layered carrot cake, p. 133
Below: Guggy cake, or huffsie, or doofie, p. 121

Victoria sponge cake

There are so many variations of this classic cake. You could make a light chocolate cake by adding 1 rounded tablespoon of cocoa mixed with 2–3 tablespoons of hot water (enough to make a thick paste) towards the end of mixing.

You can also make lamingtons, those wonderful Australian cakes: bake this mixture in a square cake tin, cut it into squares once cold, then dip each square (using two forks) into a thick chocolate butter icing and then into a dish of desiccated coconut.

You can convert it into a caramel cake by using only 125g of sugar and adding 175g of caramel or dulce de leche (about half a tin/jar). You may need an extra 5 minutes or so to bake; the cake is slightly denser.

Or you can just serve the cake in the traditional way, filled with raspberry jam and the top sprinkled with sugar – or add in a layer of buttercream or whipped cream.

It is important the butter is at room temperature before using: it should be soft enough to show a slight indentation when pressed with your finger. If you have forgotten to take the butter from the fridge, you can microwave it, but only very briefly, checking every few seconds, as it can go from hard and solid to melted in a flash.

Serves 6–8

·

175g butter, softened

175g caster sugar

3 eggs

175g self-raising flour

1 tsp baking powder

Butter and base-line two 18cm cake tins (with a depth of about 4cm). Preheat the oven to 180°C.

Place the butter and sugar in a food mixer and beat for about 5 minutes until pale. Or beat by hand with a wooden spoon for at least 10 minutes or so until creamy.

Add the eggs one at a time, adding a spoonful of the flour with each egg. Beat well, scraping down the sides of the bowl to ensure everything is incorporated. Remove the bowl from the stand, if using an electric mixer.

Gently fold in the remaining flour and baking powder with a large metal spoon, then divide the mixture between the prepared tins, smoothing out to level it off.

Bake for 20–25 minutes until springy and just firm to the touch. Leave in the tins for 5 minutes, then turn out onto a wire rack.

Leave until cold before filling.

Sultana cake

Serves 8

•

175g butter, softened

175g caster sugar

3 medium eggs

175g plain flour

pinch of salt

200g sultanas

1 – 2 tsp granulated sugar

When I lick the bowl once I have put a sultana cake in the oven, memories return of being a little girl, standing on a kitchen stool, scraping every last vestige of cake batter from the bowl of Mum's sultana cake. What did Proust know, with his dry old madeleines! Give me a moist buttery sultana cake any day.

My mum Anna Anderson's sultana cake – like her tea loaf, scones and pancakes – was available almost daily, ready to be decanted from the cake tins when people popped in, when it was teatime, or simply when the only thing that would do was cake.

There are some recipes from the eighteenth century for simple, light fruit cakes like this one; the old ones usually use currants instead of sultanas, with often an addition of some caraway seeds.

———————

Butter and base-line a deep 18cm cake tin. Preheat the oven to 170°C.

Cream the butter and sugar well together. I do this in my food mixer, but you can beat by hand. Keep going until the mixture is pale and creamy.

Beat in the eggs, one at a time, with a third of the flour after each addition. Add a pinch of salt, then stir in the sultanas and combine well.

Tip into the prepared cake tin and bake for about 1 hour, or until done (test with a cocktail stick: it should come out clean). Switch off the oven and sprinkle the top of the cake with the granulated sugar. Return to the oven for 2 – 3 minutes, then remove to a wire tray to cool.

Dundee cake (or cupcakes)

1 cake serves 8, or makes
10 cupcakes

•

175g butter, softened

175g caster sugar

grated zest of 1 large orange

3 medium eggs

175g self-raising flour

½ tsp mixed spice

pinch of salt

150g currants

150g raisins

50g chopped mixed peel

1 tbsp whisky

16–20 whole blanched
almonds

As a Dundonian, I am exceedingly proud of Dundee cake. Its origins are closely linked to the marmalade industry. The surplus of orange peel from Keiller's marmalade was used in Dundee cakes. A sign, therefore, of an authentic Dundee cake is the use of orange peel, not mixed peel. Unless you are a purist, however, mixed peel of good quality will still make a very fine cake.

The cake is a thing of great beauty, with its concentric circles of whole almonds on top. But I also love to make mini cakes, each in a muffin wrapper and studded with an almond. These are ideal for picnics, preferably on a windswept Scottish beach.

Preheat the oven to 150°C (160°C for the cupcakes).

Butter and line a deep 18cm cake tin (or place ten large paper muffin cases in a bun tin).

Cream the butter, sugar and orange zest thoroughly until light and fluffy (I do this in my food mixer), then beat in the eggs, one at a time, adding a teaspoon of the weighed flour with each egg, to prevent curdling.

Add in the rest of the flour, the mixed spice and a pinch of salt. Fold everything together gently, then stir in the dried fruits and mixed peel, together with the whisky.

For the cake, spoon the mixture into the tin, levelling the top. Bake for 1½ hours, then remove and arrange the almonds on top in two circles. Return to the oven and continue to bake for a further 45 minutes (2¼ hours altogether). Loosely cover over with foil if it looks as if it might be too dark.

If you are opting for the cupcakes, spoon the mixture into the muffin cases and add an almond to the top of each. Bake at 160°C for about 35 minutes.

To check if the cake or cupcakes are ready, insert a wooden skewer into the centre: there should be no raw batter on it when you take it out. Remove the cake or cupcakes to a wire rack to cool completely before decanting from the tin (leave the cupcakes in their paper cases).

Plum cake

This fabulous recipe is a combination of two very old Scottish ones, both beautifully written in flowery hand. One is from an anonymous book from the late seventeenth century, written in an elaborate style, with instructions for 'plume caike'. It begins 'Take 7 pounds of flower [sic]', then 'a pynt of creame and two pounds of butter'. It also has 22 eggs in it, so not a small cake!

The other is from Janet Maule's recipe book from 1701, which calls for 'a muchken of sweet cream', amongst other things. I feel an affinity with this second recipe, as Janet lived in Panmure, close to my home town of Dundee.

There is one ingredient that Janet Maule adds which is interesting; she stipulates adding 'a pound of corduidron'. This is preserved quince, from a form of the old French *condoignac*. Though the English referred to it as 'chardquynce', Scots would have preferred the French to the English word; it was before the Union in 1707. I usually add some chopped quince paste (membrillo) for extra flavour.

In Mrs MacIver's cookbook, first published in 1773, her recipe for 'Plumb-cake' includes ginger, coriander seed, caraway seed and Jamaica pepper (all-spice).

I have also found some early twentieth-century recipes for plum cake in Scotland that are similar, but often include black treacle, which would make it richer and darker. Plum cake, just like plum pudding, was a term which could refer to any cake or pudding made with raisins or other dried fruits.

This cake, which has the same basic flavourings as the old recipes (some of which from the 1700s advocate adding 'some sweetmeats if you please'), is wonderfully moist, probably due to the unusual addition of cream.

Don't be put off by the inordinate number of ingredients – it is one of the nicest fruit cakes I know, and so easy to make.

Line a deep 22cm cake tin, ensuring the paper is above the rim of the tin. Preheat the oven to 170°C.

Mix the first 11 ingredients together in a large bowl, with a pinch of salt. Beat the butter and sugar until thoroughly creamed, then beat in the eggs one by one. Stir this into the flour mixture, along with the cream and sherry.

Once well combined, spoon the mixture into the prepared tin and bake for 1 hour. Then reduce the temperature to 150°C.

Place a piece of foil loosely over the top now (or earlier, if it looks as if it's browning too much) and continue to bake for a further 1¼ hours (so, 2¼ hours altogether). Check it is cooked by inserting a skewer into the centre – it should come out clean.

Place on a wire rack to cool before removing from the tin.

Serves 10

•

400g self-raising flour

350g currants

50g raisins

50g mixed peel

grated zest of 1 lemon

grated zest of 1 small orange

75g quince paste, diced (optional)

½ tsp ground cinnamon

¼ tsp ground nutmeg

¼ tsp ground cloves

¼ tsp ground mace

pinch of salt

250g butter, softened

150g light muscovado sugar

3 eggs

100ml double cream

50ml medium sherry

Isle of Luing home bakers' bramble and apple cake

Serves 8

•

225g butter, softened

225g caster sugar

grated zest of 1 lemon

4 eggs

225g self-raising flour

225g brambles (or cultivated blackberries)

•

For the filling and top

1 medium cooking apple

1 rounded tbsp soft light brown sugar

scant ½ teaspoon ground cinnamon

1 tbsp water

100ml double cream

icing sugar, for dusting the top

On the beautiful island of Luing, off the west coast of Scotland, there is a collective of voluntary home bakers who provide cakes and traybakes for the Atlantic Island Centre in Cullipool, the largest village on Luing, and also the island shop. The baking group comprises of ten women and one man – 11 bakers out of a population of only 173 is really rather remarkable.

They also provide bakes for the weekly community lunch club, which is held at the centre out of high season and in Toberonochy village hall during the busy summer. The bread they use is baked by Mary Braithwate, who runs the wonderful Luing bakery, where she sells superb sourdough.

Mary Whitmore, my Luing friend, shared this recipe with me. She and her husband Martin collect brambles from the shores along the north of Luing and also from Ardinamir in the centre of the island.

If you have never visited Luing before, I highly recommend it. Mere minutes on the ferry from the island of Seil (which is reached by the old humpback Clachan Bridge, more commonly known as the Bridge over the Atlantic), not only is the island beautiful and peaceful but the cakes are amazing!

Butter and base-line two 20cm cake tins (not the very shallow ones). Preheat the oven to 180°C.

Cream the butter, sugar and lemon zest in a mixer until light and fluffy.

Lightly beat the eggs together, then gradually pour them into the creamed mixture, adding a spoonful or so of the flour as you go. Continue to beat well.

Fold the rest of the flour into the mixture, now using a large metal spoon. Once all is incorporated, add the brambles and fold them in with a very gentle hand: you do not want the purple juices to bleed into the cake – though it isn't a disaster if they do.

Divide between the prepared tins and smooth the tops.

Bake for about 30 minutes, or until golden and the surface springs back when lightly pressed. Remove from the oven and allow to cool for 5 – 10 minutes before turning out onto a wire rack to cool.

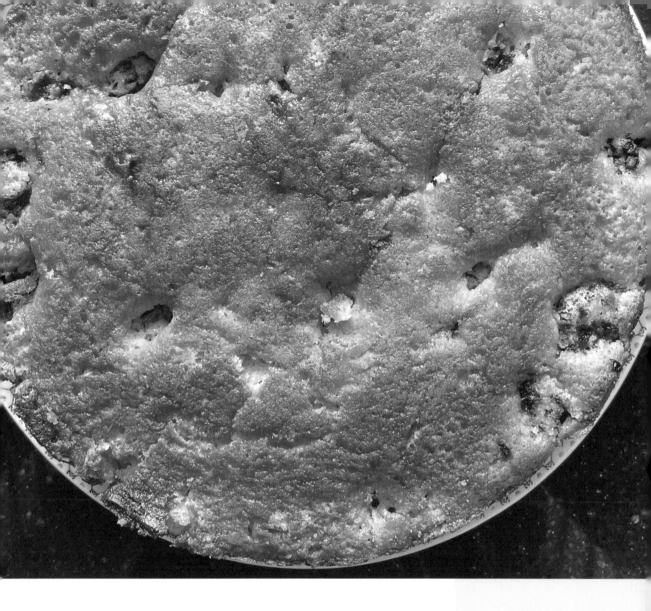

While the cake is baking, prepare the filling. Peel and core the apple and dice the flesh, then put this in a small pan with the sugar, cinnamon and water. Cover and cook gently until soft, then mash with a fork. Leave to cool.

Whip the cream until it holds its shape, then gently mix in the cooled apple.

Sandwich the cooled cakes together with the apple cream in the middle and dust the top with sifted icing sugar.

Guggy cake, or huffsie, or doofie

There are such good names for this delicious, moist cake that I could not decide which to use – so I've given three! Based on my mum's guggy cake, part of her regular teatime repertoire, it is also very similar to Whalsay's huffsie, a traditional cake from the sixth largest of the Shetland islands, and the doofie, from the south of Shetland (the Ness area, including Sumburgh, Spiggie and Bigton). In other parts of Shetland, it is called a brönnie or a brunny.

On a misty July morning in Shetland, I met up with Jenny Brown to fly to Fair Isle for the day. Having been thwarted before during a misty May some years before, I was so disappointed to once again be told the flight could not go. But the silver lining in those annoying clouds was the most wonderful walk around the Eshaness cliffs and the Holes of Scraada . . . and the delicious brönnie Jenny had brought along from the Cake Fridge on Burra, in the southern Shetland Mainland.

It's the type of cake that's often called a tea loaf in Scotland, for two reasons: first, because sometimes the dried fruit is soaked in tea; second, it is ideal served – sliced and spread with butter – with a cup of tea.

Mum's original recipe for guggy cake, from the 1950s, contained lard, but I have substituted butter. There are no eggs in it, yet it is still wonderfully moist. The black treacle adds a glorious dark hue. Remember to start an hour or so earlier than usual, to allow time for the boiled mixture to cool.

Place the first six ingredients in a heavy saucepan with the cold water. Heat gently until the butter is melted, then remove from the heat and cool.

Butter and base-line a 1kg loaf tin. Preheat the oven to 180°C.

Once the mixture is cold, add in the flour with a pinch of salt and combine well. Tip into the prepared loaf tin, levelling the surface, and bake for about 1 hour to 1 hour 5 minutes, or until a skewer inserted into the middle comes out clean. Cover loosely with foil after 30 minutes or so to prevent burning.

Remove to a wire rack to cool before turning out. Leave to cool completely before slicing and spreading thickly with butter.

Serves 8 – 10

•

100g light muscovado sugar

1 tbsp black treacle

150g sultanas

150g currants

125g butter

2 tsp mixed spice

225ml cold water

225g self-raising flour

pinch of salt

Cloutie dumpling

Serves many!

•

200g self-raising flour

150g fresh brown breadcrumbs

200g suet, shredded

1 tsp bicarbonate of soda

2 tsp mixed spice

125g light muscovado sugar

300g mixed dried fruit
(sultanas, currants, raisins)

pinch of salt

2 tbsp black treacle

300ml (approx.) whole milk

flour and caster sugar, to
sprinkle on the clout

She tried some ham and a bit of the dumpling, sugared and fine, that Mistress Melon had made. And everybody praised it, as well they might, and cried for more helpings, and more cups of tea, and there were scones and pancakes and soda-cakes and cakes made with honey that everybody ate.

This is a description of the food at Chris Guthrie's rural Aberdeenshire wedding, in the early twentieth century, from Lewis Grassic Gibbon's wonderful novel *Sunset Song*. It shows the crucial part cloutie dumplings played at special occasions.

In my Dundee family, it was made on birthdays instead of cake. And served on Christmas Day. My auntie Muriel was the one, after my granny Anderson died, to make a cloutie dumpling for members of the family on their birthdays. When I asked her for the recipe, she always said she couldn't possibly write it down, telling me there's a 'ticky of this and a ticky of that . . .': no one ever wrote cloutie dumpling recipes down, they just made them. I managed to pin her down, however, and the following recipe is based more or less on the one my family used to enjoy, with some added extras, such as the black treacle, to give it a rich, dark flavour – and less flour to make it a little lighter.

Island bakers Netta MacDougall (from Mull) and Dolina Macdonald (from Tiree) both made such delicious cloutie dumplings for me I still remember them with nostalgia years later. Those – and the one made by Catriona McGillivray on Islay – are excellent not only as puddings but also sliced and spread thickly with some butter. Catriona makes dumplings for weddings and ceilidhs all over Islay.

'Clout' or 'cloot' is Scots for cloth, and it is after the word 'cloth' that this recipe is named, as it refers to the cloth in which the dumpling is boiled. Unlike any other dumplings or steamed puddings, it forms a characteristic 'skin', made by sprinkling flour and sugar over the cloth before filling with the mixture. Beware clouties without skin, as they are not authentic. The skin must be dried off before serving and this is done nowadays in the oven.

My mother's task, as the youngest child, was to dry off the dumpling in front of the open fireplace. She would sit there on a stool for 15–20 minutes, turning the dumpling round and round until it was dried off and ready to eat.

Since it was made only for special occasions such as birthdays (in which case there were silver threepennies hidden inside, similar to charms in a Christmas pudding), this was a chore worth doing well. It would then be eaten with custard, but is now also served with cream or ice cream. Next day any leftovers would be served for breakfast: sliced and fried in rendered suet and eaten with bacon.

If you want to add coins, wrap 5 pence pieces or charms in waxed or greaseproof paper and add to the mixture.

––––––––––

Mix the first eight ingredients together in a bowl, then drizzle over the treacle. Add enough milk to give the correct consistency: you want it to be stiff yet dropping. Beat well together.

Dip a pudding cloth (or an extra large tea towel) into boiling water to scald, then drain well: I use rubber gloves to squeeze it dry. Lay it out flat on a board. Sprinkle with flour and then sugar (I use flour and sugar shakers): you want an even, but not thick, sprinkling. This forms the characteristic skin.

Now spoon the mixture into the middle of the cloth in a heap, then draw the corners of the cloth and tie up securely with string, allowing a little room for expansion. Place the cloutie on a heatproof plate in the bottom of a large saucepan. Top up with boiling water to just about cover the pudding (it must come at least three-quarters of the way up the side), then cover with a lid and simmer gently for about 3 – 3½ hours, until it feels firm.

Check the water level regularly and top up, if necessary. You should hear the reassuring, gentle shuddering sound of the plate on the bottom of the pan for the entire duration of cooking. Towards the end, preheat the oven to 180°C.

Wearing rubber gloves, remove the pudding from the pan, dip briefly into a bowl of cold water (no more than 10 seconds) so the skin does not stick to the cloth. Cut the string, untie the cloth and invert the dumpling onto a warmed ovenproof plate.

Place in the preheated oven for 10 – 15 minutes to dry off the skin – it should feel a little less sticky when removed – then sprinkle with caster sugar and serve hot with custard.

The Pierowall Hotel's mini duffs

Makes 12

•

175g self-raising flour

175g fresh breadcrumbs

175ml sunflower oil

125g soft brown sugar

1 tsp baking soda

2 tsp ground cinnamon

1 tsp ground ginger

2 tbsp golden syrup

450g dried fruit
(raisins/sultanas/currants)

1 apple, peeled, cored,
finely chopped

250ml milk

On the beautiful island of Westray, in the Orkney isles, there is a wonderful hotel in Pierowall, the main village. The hotel is run by Mabel Kent, who used to be the cook at the island school 3 minutes along the road before she took over the hotel in 2019.

Mabel is one of that rare breed of brilliant cooks (she would not call herself a chef) who not only provides excellent food at breakfast, lunch and dinner in the hotel's small dining room, but does so using local produce where at all possible. Her menus always include locally landed fish, from the island's Pierowall Fish just across the bay from the hotel. Her beef is from Orkney, and she uses Scottish lamb.

Mabel and her husband, Brian, grow their own vegetables in the garden at the back of the hotel – the tatties grown are made into hand-cut chips, which are legendary.

One of her best-loved puddings is what she calls 'duffs' – the name more commonly used on the Scottish islands for cloutie dumplings. Mabel used to make one large duff for groups of senior citizens who came to the hotel for lunch every two weeks. There were 12 of them, so just one batch was made . . . but they all wanted the outside piece of the duff, with its characteristic skin, so that's when she decided to make one mini duff per person.

The mixture she uses can also be made into one large cloutie, in which case boil it for 3–4 hours.

Mix everything together, then divide between 12 small damp cloths that have a sprinkling of flour on them (prepare the cloths as per the Cloutie dumpling recipe on page 122).

Tie up each mini duff with string, leaving a little room for expansion. I like to place them on a large plate, like the Cloutie dumpling recipe, in a pot of simmering water for about 1½ hours.

Then, once done, carefully remove each cloth and let them sit on a plate; the characteristic skin forms as they begin to cool.

Serve with custard.

Cherry and almond cake

Most recipes for cherry cake advise quartering the glacé cherries so they are lighter and do not sink into the cake; they are also rinsed to make them devoid of their heavy syrupy coating. Most recipes also advise coating in flour to prevent sinking. But all I like to do is wash and – thoroughly – dry them, then, instead of mixing into the cake batter, I add the cherries once I've filled the tin with half of the batter, then pour the rest on top. This means every wedge of cake will have nice big whole cherries sitting all plump and round in the centre of it.

You can use the natural coloured glacé cherries, as the red colouring is unnecessary. However, if you want the old-fashioned look of a pillar-box red-studded moist golden cake, then go for the regular ones. I use orange juice in the cake mix if it's for family teatime; rum, if it's aimed at adults.

If you want to emphasise the almond theme, you can also arrange 20 whole blanched almonds on the surface of the cake, once it's ready for the oven, in the style of a Dundee cake.

This cake will keep, well wrapped in foil, for up to two weeks.

Serves 8

•

200g glacé cherries

175g butter, softened

175g caster sugar

3 medium eggs

175g self-raising flour

pinch of salt

100g ground almonds

1 – 2 tbsp orange juice
or dark rum

Butter and base-line a deep, round, 18cm cake tin. Preheat the oven to 170°C.

First rinse the cherries in a colander, then pat thoroughly dry on several sheets of kitchen paper; it's important that they are really dry, so do this well in advance if possible and keep patting dry.

Beat the butter and sugar until light and fluffy – up to 5 minutes in a food mixer or double that by hand. You can also use a hand-held electric whisk. Break in the eggs, one by one, stirring after each and adding a spoonful of the flour after one or two, as it will probably look a little curdled.

Now, using a large metal spoon (not the food mixer), gently fold in the remaining flour by hand, with a pinch of salt and the ground almonds. Finally, add enough juice or rum to make a soft but thick batter.

Spoon just over half the mixture into the prepared cake tin. Arrange the whole cherries all over that before topping with the remaining batter, spreading gently out to level the surface.

Bake in the preheated oven for 1 hour 20 – 25 minutes, covering loosely with foil for the last 10 – 20 minutes to prevent burning. Test by inserting a wooden cocktail stick into the centre: it should come out clean. The edges of the cake will also have shrunk slightly from the sides of the tin.

Remove the cake and leave for half an hour or so, then run a knife around the edges and decant onto a wire rack to cool completely.

Lemon curd polenta cake

The polenta in this lovely yellow cake makes the texture slightly gritty and the flavour from the lemon curd is wonderfully tangy. There is also a good background hint of olive oil – I recommend using a fruity oil, not a peppery one, if possible. It's worth reading the label on the bottle.

This is good served as it is, with a cup of tea, or as a pudding, barely warm, with some whipped cream and a dollop of lemon curd.

Serves 8

•

75g fine polenta

150g self-raising flour

¼ tsp baking powder

100g caster sugar

pinch of salt

3 medium eggs

3 tbsp (fruity) olive oil

3 tbsp lemon curd
(preferably home-made)

Butter a square 18cm cake tin. Preheat the oven to 200°C.

Place the polenta, flour, baking powder and sugar in a bowl with a pinch of salt. Stir to combine.

In a separate bowl, whisk the eggs and oil together until thick, then add to the dry ingredients, along with the lemon curd. Fold everything together gently until thoroughly combined.

Spoon into the prepared tin.

Bake for 10 minutes, then lower the heat to 180°C and continue to bake for a further 15 minutes or so, until a cocktail stick inserted into the middle comes out clean.

Transfer the tin to a wire rack to cool, then cut into squares.

Orange and hazelnut cake

Serves 8

•

1 medium orange (weighing
about 200g)

175g butter, softened

175g light muscovado sugar

150g self-raising flour

75g ground and
chopped roasted hazelnuts
(I like 50g ground +
25g chopped, but you
can use all ground)

3 medium eggs

½ tsp bicarbonate of soda

This delicious, moist cake is based on a recipe by wonderful home baker Maggie Darling.

Maggie usually uses ground almonds, but has also used hazelnuts – and even pistachios. And sometimes she adds poppy or chia seeds. It is the easiest ever cake, as everything is just placed in a food processor and whizzed together. The only hard part is waiting till it cools before eating.

It can be iced with a delicious cream cheese frosting, made with 400g cream cheese, half a small tub of mascarpone, 250g sifted icing sugar and a tablespoon or two (enough to make a smooth icing) of orange juice. Spread this over the cake once cooled.

Butter and base-line a deep 23cm round cake tin. Preheat the oven to 190°C.

Cut off and discard the ends from the orange, then cut the rest into about eight pieces, removing and discarding the pips. Place everything else – skin/pith/flesh – in a food processor. Process to a fine sludge.

Add the butter, sugar, flour, hazelnuts, eggs and bicarbonate of soda and process briefly for about 15 seconds, stopping halfway through and scraping down the sides.

Tip into the prepared tin and bake for 25 – 30 minutes, or until a wooden cocktail stick inserted into the middle comes out clean. Cool for 20 minutes or so in the tin before turning out onto a wire rack.

Apple streusel cake

This is based on a recipe for *Apfel-streusel-kuchen* that I used to love during my years living in northern Germany. You can also make it with plums or rhubarb (for plums, stone and chop the fruit; for rhubarb, clean it and cut it into chunks).
Made with gluten-free flour, it has a lovely, almost crunchy bite to it.

Butter and base-line an 18cm springform cake tin. Preheat the oven to 190°C.

Melt the butter in large bowl in the microwave or in a large pan over a low heat. Remove from the heat and add the caster sugar, mixing well, then stir in the flour and egg. Place two-thirds of this mixture into the prepared tin, pressing out gently with floured hands to cover the base.

Peel, core and slice the apples, then mix these in a bowl with the raisins, cinnamon and demerara sugar. Tip this into the tin, pressing down gently.

Using floured hands, place the remaining dough over the top in tiny clumps – tear off small pieces and crumble it between your fingers over the apples. Again, press down gently with floured hands.

Bake for about 50 minutes until cooked through, covering loosely with foil after about half an hour.

Cool in the tin for about 20 minutes, then decant carefully onto a board or plate. Serve warm or cold.

Serves 8

•

100g butter

100g caster sugar

200g self-raising flour

1 egg, beaten

500 – 600g cooking apples
(2 extra large or 3 large)

75g raisins

1 tsp ground cinnamon

75g demerara sugar

Windfall apple sauce cake

Serves 8

•

125g butter, softened

50g caster sugar

4 rounded tbsp apple sauce

150g self-raising flour

¼ tsp bicarbonate of soda

pinch of salt

½ teaspoon ground cinnamon

1 egg, beaten

50g hazelnuts, chopped

I lived in Ostfriesland, in northern Germany, for nearly three years in my late 20s, and one of my favourite things to eat there was *apfelmus* (thick apple sauce), which you could buy in jars. I would add it to cakes, mix it with yoghurt, top porridge with it, spoon it into hungry babies and just eat it neat from the jar. I make it often now during early autumn, as the windfall apples fall from our neighbour's garden into ours.

This is a delicious, moist cake that can be served as it is with a cup of tea, or as a pudding with caramelised apples and thick yoghurt.

To cook the apples, it is difficult to give measurements, as windfalls are by nature invariably bruised and so you have to cut away some of the flesh once peeled. But you will need at least six large cooking apples, peeled and chopped. I put these into a large bowl with a sprinkling of sugar (3–4 teaspoons) and cook in the microwave for 8–10 minutes until completely soft (you can also cook in a pan, but you will need a couple of tablespoons of water). Drain over a sieve and tip the apples into a food processor with a good dod* of butter, then puree until thick and smooth. It is the butter that gives the wonderfully rich, creamy texture.

Butter and base-line a deep, 18cm springform cake tin. Preheat the oven to 180°C.

Beat the butter and sugar until creamy, then stir in the apple sauce. Mix in the flour, bicarbonate of soda, pinch of salt and cinnamon, then add the egg and nuts. Stir everything together to combine.

Tip into the prepared tin and bake for 45 – 50 minutes, or until a wooden cocktail stick inserted into the middle comes out clean.

Leave in the tin for half an hour or so, then transfer to a wire rack.

* a 'dod' in Scotland is a knob of butter

Two-layered carrot cake

This is based on a couple of recipes – my original Carrot cake (p. 134), and that of one of the brilliant Isle of Luing home bakers, Avril Buchanan. Avril's cake is two-layered and has this wonderful icing, with whipped cream enriching the cream cheese. It is a great favourite on the island.

Because of the cream, keep it refrigerated once iced.

Butter and base-line two 20cm cake tins. Preheat the oven to 160°C.

Peel the carrots and cut off the ends. Finely grate them, then pat really dry in kitchen paper. The resulting weight should be about 225g.

Place them in a food mixer with all the remaining ingredients and beat for 2–3 minutes until well combined. (Or beat it all together by hand.) Pour into the two tins and bake for about 30 minutes, or until the cakes are done. Test them by inserting a wooden cocktail stick into the centre. It should come out clean.

Leave the cakes for 15–20 minutes in their tins, then carefully invert onto a wire rack to cool.

For the icing, place the cream cheese in a food mixer and beat well until smooth. (Or beat by hand.) Add the icing sugar and beat well until thoroughly combined, then add the cream, beating for a minute or two until it has the consistency of thick cream that holds its shape.

Use a third of the mixture to sandwich the cakes together, then pile the remainder on to the top of the cake, smoothing with a palette knife. Decorate with the nuts.

Serves 8–10

•

350g carrots (unpeeled weight)

225g light muscovado sugar

225g self-raising flour

225ml sunflower oil

4 medium eggs

50g chopped walnuts

75g raisins

1 tsp ground cinnamon

1 tsp mixed spice

grated zest of 1 small orange

•

For the topping & filling

280g tub of cream cheese

150g icing sugar, sifted

75ml double cream

handful of chopped walnuts, to decorate

Carrot cake

Serves 8

•

250g carrots
(unpeeled weight)

150g light muscovado sugar

150ml vegetable oil

3 eggs, beaten

150g self-raising flour

1 rounded tsp ground
cinnamon

grating of nutmeg (optional)

1 tsp bicarbonate of soda

100g raisins

•

For the lemon glacé icing

100g icing sugar, sifted

1 tbsp fresh lemon juice

•

For the cream cheese icing

100g butter, softened

½ tsp vanilla extract

175g icing sugar, sifted

100g cream cheese

handful of chopped walnuts

This cake is based on my father-in-law John Lawrence's recipe. Though, like my husband, he was a pilot, his family were bakers and it must have been in the blood, as he made a mean carrot cake, iced with a simple, light lemony glacé icing, which was a great family favourite. John always flavoured the cake with plenty of nutmeg, but I prefer the more gentle hit of cinnamon, but do add, if you enjoy the flavour of nutmeg.

I also love carrot cake with a cream cheese icing, so have given both possibilities here.

———

Butter and base-line a round, 18cm-deep cake tin. Preheat the oven to 180°C.

Peel and finely grate the carrots. (It is important they are not coarsely grated.) Pat them dry on kitchen paper.

Using a balloon whisk, whip together the sugar and oil, then gradually whisk in the eggs.

Combine the flour, cinnamon, nutmeg (if using) and bicarbonate of soda, and fold these into the mixture, using a large metal spoon.

Stir in the carrots and raisins and combine thoroughly.

Tip the mixture into the prepared cake tin and bake for about 40 minutes or until well risen and firm to the touch; a skewer inserted to the middle should come out clean. Cover lightly with foil, if you need to bake further.

Remove the tin to a wire rack. Cool in the tin for about half an hour, then carefully invert onto the wire rack to cool completely before icing.

For the glacé icing, sift the icing sugar into a bowl, then beat in the lemon juice. Once smooth, pour over the cake and allow it to drizzle down the sides.

For the cream cheese icing, beat the butter until smooth, then add the vanilla extract, mixing it in well. Gradually add the sifted icing sugar (covering with a tea towel if you are using a food mixer, as clouds of icing sugar dust will go everywhere). Once thoroughly mixed, add the cream cheese, but don't beat now, rather just gently mix till all are combined and thick. Use to decorate the top of the cake, swirling with a knife, if you like.

Top with a handful of chopped walnuts to finish.

Sticky toffee apple cake with coconut crunch

This squidgy apple cake has the most delectable crunchy coconut topping. It not only looks amazing, but also tastes divine. My friend Isabelle's daughter, Jess Plews, told me about enjoying a piece of cake called a lumberjack cake in her local café when she used to live in Brighton and I thought the ingredients would appeal greatly to our Scottish sweet tooth.

It is like sticky toffee pudding and bounty bar (without the chocolate coating) rolled into one delicious moist cake. Have it cold with a cup of tea, or barely warm with thick cream for pudding. I defy you to stop at one slice.

Butter and base-line a deep 24cm loose-bottomed cake tin. It must be at least 10cm deep. Preheat the oven to 180°C.

Place the dates in a large, heavy saucepan with the bicarbonate of soda and 250ml of boiling water. Heat on low for 4–5 minutes until the dates are softened. Add the apples, then remove from the heat and stir in the butter. Once it has melted, add the sugars and flour, then, once thoroughly but gently combined, stir in the eggs.

Pour into the prepared cake tin. Bake on a foil-lined baking tray (in case of spillage) for 30 minutes.

While it is baking, place the first five topping ingredients in another pan and bring slowly to the boil. Let it bubble away, stirring for 2–3 minutes, then add in the coconut and remove from the heat.

After the cake has baked for 30 minutes, remove the tray carefully and place on top of the cooker. Spoon the coconut mixture all over the top – you must do this slowly, so that the cake does not collapse with a sudden surge! Once done, place back in the oven and continue to bake for a further 30 minutes until cooked through, covering loosely with foil after 15 minutes or so to prevent burning. It bakes for about 1 hour altogether.

Remove, cool, then carefully transfer to a serving plate.

Serves 8–10

•

175g stoned dates, chopped

1 tsp bicarbonate of soda

250ml boiling water

2 crisp, green eating apples (such as Granny Smith), peeled and chopped

100g butter, diced

100g caster sugar

75g light muscovado sugar

250g self-raising flour

2 medium eggs, beaten

•

For the coconut crunch topping

75g butter

150g light muscovado sugar

100ml double cream

1 tsp vanilla extract

1 tbsp golden syrup

100g shredded coconut (or half desiccated/half coconut flakes)

Tosca cake

My dad, Bob Anderson, worked with Carlsberg and travelled a lot to Copenhagen. Every time he returned, he would tell us about the marvellous paintings in the Glyptotek museum, the warmth of the Danes' hospitality – and, of course, the delicious food.

I was given my parents' Danish cookbook and the one page I turn to again and again is the recipe for Tosca cake. Mine is based on the famous Danish *Toscakage* – similar to Sweden's *Toscakaka* – a buttery lemon sponge topped with crunchy almonds.

It can be served with coffee – or for pudding, with clotted cream and seasonal berries.

Butter a 24cm springform cake tin. Preheat the oven to 170°C.

Cream together the butter and sugar with the lemon zest until light and fluffy, then gradually add the eggs, one at a time, beating well after each addition. Fold in the flour, then tip the mixture into the cake tin. Smooth the top, then bake for 20 minutes until firm.

Meanwhile, make the topping. Melt the butter, then stir in the remaining ingredients. Just before the 20 minutes is up and the cake is just firm, bring the mixture to the boil, then pour immediately over the cake, smoothing out.

Return to the oven and bake for a further 20 minutes, or until it is golden brown.

Leave for 20 – 30 minutes before decanting. Serve warm.

Serves 8

•

150g butter, softened

150g caster sugar

grated zest of 1 lemon

2 eggs

100g self-raising flour

•

For the topping

100g butter

100g granulated sugar

100g chopped almonds

1 rounded tbsp plain flour

2 tbsp double cream

Broonie

Serves 10

•

150g medium oatmeal

200g self-raising flour

2 tsp ground ginger

2 rounded tbsp black treacle

125g butter, diced

100g light muscovado sugar

1 egg, beaten

150ml buttermilk
(or natural yoghurt –
the runny variety, not set)

The Orcadian broonie should not to be confused with Shetland's 'fatty brunnies', which are thick girdle scones or bannocks made of wholemeal flour or oatmeal. Yule brunnies in Shetland were made from rye flour and their edges were 'nipped out to represent the sun's rays'. There is also the Shetland brönnie, another name for the famous Shetland huffsie (see page 121).

The names brunnie and broonie are from the old Norse word *bruni*, which, according to writer F. Marian McNeill, means a thick bannock. In her broonie recipe in *The Scots Kitchen* (1929), she rubs the butter into the oatmeal and flour. I prefer melting the butter with the treacle and sugar, as we do in most gingerbreads. She also has equal parts oatmeal to flour; I prefer a little less oatmeal, as it can be rather dry otherwise.

The Orkney broonie is a moist, oaty gingerbread not dissimilar to Yorkshire or Lancashire parkin, which is traditionally served on Bonfire Night. Dorothy Hartley, in her seminal work *Food in England* (1954), has a good parkin recipe that includes mixed peel. She also advocates serving it as a pudding with apple sauce: 'When making parkin, it was popular in the north country to make an extra panful to serve hot, smothered with apple sauce, at tea-time.'

And if that doesn't sound delicious enough, chef Neil Forbes, owner of the fabulous Café St Honoré in Edinburgh, makes his broonie with porridge oats, not oatmeal, then serves it warm, in the style of sticky toffee pudding, with butterscotch sauce and a drizzle of double cream.

I like to go the extra mile and warm up thick slices, then serve them flooded with hot butterscotch sauce and a great dollop of clotted cream and/or a generous scoop of vanilla ice cream, for a truly memorable pudding.

The broonie keeps well, wrapped in foil, and is good either plain or buttered with a cup of tea.

Combine the oatmeal, flour and ginger in a bowl.

Place the treacle, butter and sugar in a small pan (or microwave bowl) and heat very gently over a low heat (or in the microwave for a minute or so) until melted, then leave to cool slightly.

Butter a 1kg loaf tin and base-line with baking parchment. Preheat the oven to 170°C.

Pour the treacle mixture into the flour mixture, stir to combine, then add the beaten egg and buttermilk (or yoghurt).

Stir gently until thoroughly combined, then tip into the prepared tin.

Bake in the preheated oven for about 50 minutes or until a skewer inserted into the middle comes out clean. (Start testing at 40 minutes.)

Leave the broonie in the tin for half an hour or so, then decant onto a wire rack. Allow it to become completely cold before cutting.

Gingerbread

Serves 10

·

200g butter

200g dark muscovado sugar

225g black treacle (half a tin)

250g plain flour

2 rounded teaspoons
ground ginger

pinch of salt

2 medium eggs, beaten

1 tsp bicarbonate of soda

75ml tepid milk

The rich, dark cake we know nowadays as gingerbread has its origins as a hard ginger biscuit, flavoured with spices and dotted with dried fruit. Nowadays there are many regional gingerbreads throughout Scotland, from Kirriemuir and Fochabers to Orkney, all made with a variety of ingredients.

This is a recipe for a gently spiced, treacly and delectably moist cake that is divine as it is, or each slice spread thickly with butter. It keeps well wrapped in foil.

———————

Butter and line a 1kg loaf tin. Preheat the oven to 170°C.

Heat the first three ingredients in a pan over a low heat until liquid. Do not boil. Cool for a few minutes.

Meanwhile place the flour, ginger and pinch of salt into a big bowl. Make a well in the centre and add the eggs.

Dissolve the bicarbonate of soda in the tepid milk and add this to the 'well'. Slowly pour in the treacle mixture and combine everything thoroughly together.

Tip into the prepared loaf tin and place in the oven for about 1 hour, covering loosely with foil after 15–20 minutes. It is done when a wooden cocktail stick, pushed in, comes out almost clean; it can have a little moist crumb.

Remove to a wire rack. Leave until completely cold before decanting from the tin and cutting.

Whisky fruit cake

This is the most moist, moreish – and boozy – fruit cake imaginable. It is far from those cakes that might look gorgeous but, once opened, are in fact disappointingly dry and crumbly. The dried fruit for this cake is soaked overnight in whisky, so it is plumped up and the flavour redolent of Scotland's national drink.

Obviously the flavour depends on what type of whisky you use – an Islay will lend more of a peaty tang than a Highland. I am no connoisseur, but I would suggest you use a whisky you also like to drink in a dram, so preferably malt. Though since you need a fair amount of whisky, blended is also just fine.

This keeps well – wrapped in foil and tucked away in a tin – for a good couple of weeks. It is ideal to offer with a cup of tea, or a dram with perhaps a slice of cheddar on the side, such as Mull Cheddar – or to take on a picnic. For the latter, do remember to warn the driver it is rather redolent of whisky!

Soak the first five ingredients in the whisky overnight. (If it is really warm – unlikely in Scotland – I put it into the fridge, then bring it back to room temperature well before mixing.)

Next day, butter and line a 23cm-deep cake tin. I like to line the sides of the tin with lining paper above the depth of the tin to protect the surface from burning. Preheat the oven to 170°C.

Cream the butter and sugar together until soft and light. Add the eggs one by one, then tip in all the fruit (which will by now have absorbed all the whisky).

Add in the flour, baking powder and spice, along with the almonds, combining well.

Spoon into the lined cake tin.

Bake for 1¾ – 2 hours, or until done, covering loosely with foil for the last half hour or so to prevent burning. Test by inserting a skewer into the centre: it should come out clean.

Remove to a wire rack and leave until completely cold, then invert.

Serves 10

•

250g sultanas

250g raisins

250g currants

100g mixed peel

50g glacé cherries

400ml whisky

150g butter, softened

150g light muscovado sugar

3 eggs

200g plain flour

1 tsp baking powder

2 tsp mixed spice

25g ground almonds

Orkney fudge cheesecake

Serves 8 – 10

•

250g Hobnobs
(or other oaty biscuits)

75g butter

300g full-fat cream cheese

300g Orkney fudge, chilled

450ml double cream

Any visitor to Orkney over the past couple of decades will have been unable to leave the islands without trying what has become a local institution – the Orkney fudge cheesecake. Rich and creamy, it is made with local fudge and is possibly the most moreish cheesecake ever.

If you can't find Orkney fudge, use another good quality fudge. I have even used tablet for this and it works pretty well, too.

It is easier to grate the fudge if it is well chilled first.

Decorate with extra grated fudge or with seasonal berries.

Lightly butter a 24cm springform cake tin.

Make the base by first crushing the biscuits and melting the butter, then combining the two well together. Press the mixture into the base of the cake tin.

Beat the cream cheese until soft.

Grate the fudge: I find this easiest using a food processor.

Tip most of the fudge into the cream cheese, leaving a tablespoon or so for garnish. Combine well. Lightly whip the cream, then gently fold it into the cream cheese mixture, combining everything together slowly.

Spoon over the base, level it off with a palette knife and cover. Chill for at least 6 hours before scattering the remaining fudge on top.

Carefully decant the cheesecake and serve in wedges.

Gooseberry and elderflower cheesecake

Serves 10

•

For the base

175g ginger nut/snap biscuits

175g digestive biscuits

100g butter

•

For the filling

350g curd (or cream) cheese

2 eggs

juice of 1 small lemon

125g caster sugar

350g gooseberries, topped and tailed

2 tbsp elderflower cordial

•

For the topping

200ml crème fraîche

50g caster sugar

I remember one of my friend's gardens had gooseberry bushes; I never understood their appeal. Our garden had raspberries and blackcurrants and, of course, rhubarb, all of which were used in jam, jelly and crumbles. But, as a child, gooseberries, even when cooked into pies and crumbles, never filled me with joy.

As an adult, however, I adore them. I love combining them in sweet dishes with elderflower, and sweet cicely in savoury sauces to accompany an oily fish, such as mackerel or herring.

This delicious pudding is rich and moreish . . . you have been warned!

———

Lightly butter a deep, 24cm loose-based cake tin. Preheat the oven to 180°C.

Process the biscuits into crumbs, then melt the butter. Mix together and press into the buttered tin, pushing up the sides too. Chill.

Beat together the curd (cream) cheese, eggs, lemon juice and 100g of the caster sugar with a balloon whisk. When it is smooth, pour into the chilled biscuit base and place on a baking sheet in the preheated oven for 30 minutes, then remove.

Meanwhile, cook the gooseberries with the remaining 25g of sugar and 1 tablespoon of cordial for about 10 minutes or until soft. Remove from the heat and drain the gooseberries in a sieve over a small pan.

Boil these reserved juices for 5 – 10 minutes until reduced to about 1 tablespoon. Place this in a bowl with the drained berries and the remaining tablespoon of cordial. Stir, then mash roughly with a potato masher. Leave to cool.

Once the cheesecake is cool, carefully spread the gooseberry filling over the top.

For the topping, beat the crème fraîche and sugar together, then pour this slowly over the gooseberries. Return to the oven and continue to bake for a further 20 minutes or so, then turn the oven off but leave the cheesecake inside for an hour at least. This helps prevent cracks.

Once out of the oven, allow to become completely cool before slicing.

Cookie Shine cake

A 'cookie shine' is old Scots for a tea party. Used mainly in the nineteenth century, the term is more or less obsolete these days, but I have named this cake after it, as it is so full of gorgeous things it is worthy of a party. It would make an excellent birthday cake.

Cookies in Scotland do not mean those massive American biscuits; rather they are the round, yeasted sweet buns, usually either split and filled with cream, or iced (with often garishly coloured icing) and known as iced cookies.

I was delighted that in the wonderful Craigard Kitchen, in Ballygrant on Islay, owner Nicola Fitz-Hardy bakes Cookie Shine cake regularly, using my recipe. She has run the café since January 2022 and her bakes are legendary. Her Cookie Shine cake looks much better than mine, as she pipes on the icing. She says it's one of her best-sellers – praise indeed on an island of excellent bakers.

Butter two 20cm cake tins. Preheat the oven to 180°C.

For the cake, mix the flour, sugar, cinnamon and a pinch of salt together, then add the eggs and oil. Add the pineapple (only the fruit, discard – or drink! – the juices), bananas, coconut and nuts. Combine well, spoon into the two cake tins and bake for 35 – 40 minutes, or until a skewer comes out clean.

Leave for 20 – 30 minutes, then turn onto a wire rack to cool.

For the icing, cream the butter, vanilla and cream cheese together with electric beaters until smooth, then sift in the icing sugar a little at a time. Beat again until completely smooth.

Use to fill and top the cake, then scatter the remaining hazelnuts over the top.

Serves 8

•

250g self-raising flour

275g light muscovado sugar

½ tsp ground cinnamon

pinch of salt

2 eggs, beaten

225ml sunflower oil

1 × can (432g) crushed pineapple in natural juice, drained thoroughly over a sieve

2 small ripe bananas, mashed

50g desiccated coconut

75g chopped, roasted hazelnuts + extra to decorate

•

For the icing

100g butter, softened

1 tsp vanilla extract

200g cream cheese

300g icing sugar

Chocolate Coca-Cola cake

This is a wonderfully moist, rich chocolate cake. Inspired by a recipe in an American 'bake sale' book, this version makes a good birthday cake, with its dark fudge chocolate icing. You will need almost one regular can of Coke for this recipe – and while I loathe Coke to drink, I have to admit it makes a truly excellent cake that everyone – adults and children alike – adore.

Butter a deep, 24cm springform cake tin. Preheat the oven to 180°C.

Place the flour, cocoa and bicarbonate of soda into a bowl, then stir in the caster sugar.

Slowly melt the butter with the Coca-Cola in a saucepan, then add this slowly to the dry mixture, with the milk, eggs and vanilla, stirring all the time.

Once thoroughly (but gently) combined, tip the mixture into the buttered tin and bake for about 40 minutes or until a skewer comes out clean. Leave on a wire rack for 10 minutes or so, then loosen off and remove the sides. Cool on its base on the rack.

For the icing, melt the butter in a pan, then mix in the Coca-Cola and cocoa.

Sift the icing sugar into a bowl, then pour the liquid over it, stirring or beating really well until smooth.

Once the cake is completely cold, remove it carefully to a plate and top with the icing.

Serves 10

•

250g self-raising flour

3 rounded tbsp cocoa powder

¼ tsp bicarbonate of soda

275g caster sugar

200g butter

250ml Coca-Cola

100ml milk

2 eggs

1 tsp vanilla extract

•

For the icing

150g butter

50ml Coca-Cola

3 rounded tbsp cocoa powder

400g icing sugar

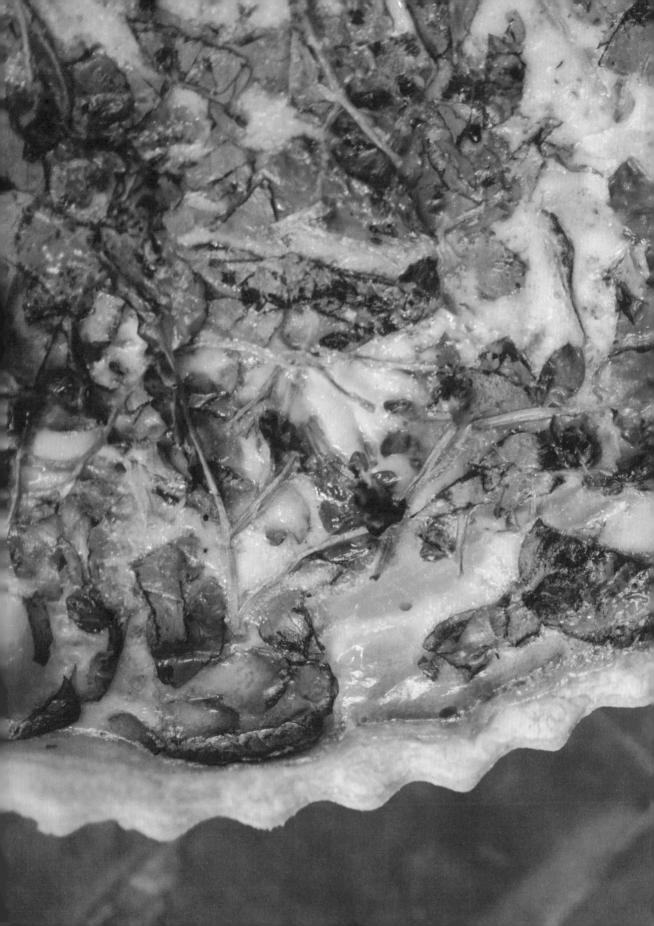

6
Savoury tarts, quiches & pies

Mince round

Meat pie

Smoked haddock tart

Artichoke and Mull Cheddar tart

Tomato and Stornoway black pudding tart

Spinach, feta and mint filo rolls

Corra Linn cheese and saffron filo tartlets

Classic Quiche Lorraine

Asparagus and mint tart

Partan bree tart

Haggis tartlets with red onion marmalade

Forfar bridies

Venison bridies

Cullen skink bridies

Meatloaf pie

Corned beef meringue pie

Vol-au-vents (with prawn or mushrooms)

Cheese straws

Westray Wife and caramelised red onion quiche

Hot smoked salmon and watercress tart

Introduction

As a child, pies were always savoury, tarts were always sweet. There was no such thing as a quiche – and a mince round was neither a tart nor a pie. Nowadays, nomenclature is even more confusing.

Regional variations for fillings encased or based on pastry in Scotland are endless. With Dundonian parents, in my family a pie meant a mutton (or beef) pie, the individual Scotch pie with a lid often eaten at football matches, when the grease would invariably run down your chin! This pie was often served at Saturday lunchtime to the non-match-goers in Dundee too, with baked beans as the accompanying 'vegetable'.

There was also the steak pie, basically a slow-cooked beef stew topped, and usually based, in puff pastry and served with great ceremony on New Year's Day.

Tarts were sweet: an apple tart, say, made in a shallow tin or enamel plate, with pastry top and bottom; or a deep individual rhubarb tart, with sticky pink juices dribbling seductively down the sides.

Quiche made its appearance in the 1960s and 1970s and, to be honest, life has never been quite the same.

Good tarts, pies and quiches rely on good pastry and it really is not at all hard to do.

Previous page: Hot smoked salmon and watercress tart, p. 181
Below: Tomato and Stornoway black pudding tart, p. 156

Mince round

A mince round is a wonderfully Scottish dish of best mince encased in pastry and baked on a flat pie plate. It is not – I repeat, *not* – a Scotch pie, with its glorious hot-water crust shaped into a deep individual pie; nor is it a steak pie, with its golden puff pastry topping and chunky gravy-filled steak filling.

Many butchers make their mince rounds with puff pastry, like steak pie, but I have always preferred shortcrust. My recipe has pastry that is nicely short, with the addition of a little vinegar, and a filling that is delightfully savoury and homely. Be sure to make it with only the best quality steak mince.

In order to finely chop the onion, carrot and mushrooms, I often cheat and sling them in the food processor and blitz with the pulse button until just done – but take care you do not over-process them, or you will end up with an oniony puree

---

First make the pastry. Place the flour, butter and a good pinch of salt in a food processor and whizz until it resembles breadcrumbs. While the machine is running, add the vinegar and about 75ml cold water (enough for it to combine together). Do not over-process. Gather into a ball, wrap in cling film and chill.

For the filling, heat the oil in a pan and fry the onion, carrot and mushrooms for a few minutes, stirring, then add the mince and cook, stirring occasionally, for 4–5 minutes until broken up and browned.

Add the tomato puree, stir well, then add the flour and stir until combined. Next, add the Worcestershire sauce and stock, and a good grinding of pepper. Bring to the boil, stir well, then reduce the heat and cook, uncovered, for about 10 minutes or until thick. Add salt and pepper to taste. Tip into a bowl and leave to chill completely.

Meanwhile, butter a 23cm metal pie plate really well. Preheat the oven to 200°C.

Roll out two-thirds of the pastry to a round, then use this to line the pie plate. Spoon in the cooled filling, then roll out the remaining pastry and use to cover the filling, trimming around the sides and crimping the edges together between your forefinger and thumb. Using scissors, make two slits in the middle, then glaze, using a pastry brush, with the egg.

Bake in the oven for about 50 minutes, covering loosely with foil for the last 20 minutes or so, if necessary, to prevent burning.

Once golden, remove, leave for at least 10 minutes, then cut and serve hot, in slices, with green vegetables.

Serves 6

•

For the pastry

300g plain flour

175g butter, chilled, diced

good pinch of salt

1 tsp white wine vinegar

75ml (approx.) cold water

•

For the filling

2 tbsp olive oil

1 small/medium onion, peeled and finely chopped

1 medium carrot, peeled and finely chopped

100g button mushrooms, wiped clean and finely chopped

500g steak mince

2 tbsp tomato puree

1 tbsp plain flour

2 tbsp Worcestershire sauce

200ml beef stock, hot

a grinding of black pepper

salt and pepper, to taste

1 small egg, lightly beaten, to glaze

Meat pie

Makes 4

•

For the beef stew

25g butter

olive oil, for frying

450g stewing beef (such as chuck), diced

2 tbsp plain flour, seasoned with salt and pepper

1 medium onion, peeled and finely chopped

2 small carrots, peeled and diced

300ml beef stock, hot

1 rounded tbsp tomato puree

1 tbsp Worcestershire sauce

•

For the pastry

50g strong white flour

75g plain flour

60g butter, diced

2 tbsp cold water

•

175g ready-rolled puff pastry

1 egg, beaten

The idea for this pie comes from two places: Scotland and Australia. First, Scotland. On New Year's Day, we traditionally serve up steak pie; indeed, it used to be served on Christmas Day in many families. It is a thick, chunky beef stew covered in puff pastry accompanied with mashed potatoes and often marrowfat (or mushy) peas – known as buster peas in my home town of Dundee.

The second connection, the Australian one, is that in Adelaide there used to be pie carts that set up in the city each evening serving Pie Floaters. There are many claims to the origin of the Pie Floater – but some insist it was 'invented' by a Scottish immigrant in the 1880s.

By the early 2000s, there were only two pie carts left, though in their heyday there had been about 30. On my last trip to that gourmet city some 20 years ago, I arrived eagerly at one of them and opted for a delicious Mini Floater, a smaller version of the mighty Pie Floater. I was not disappointed.

The meat pies from the pie carts were filled with chunky beef, but, unlike our Scottish steak pie, it had a shortcrust base, as well as a puff pastry top. Another discerning factor was that just before serving a Pie Floater the pie was inverted, piping hot, into a dish and a flood of thick pea soup ladled on top; it was then finished off with a skoosh of tomato ketchup. It was usually taken late at night – often as an antidote to excess alcohol – and it was not unusual to see party-goers, sometimes in black tie and long dresses, standing at tables set up beside the carts with their plastic spoons, tucking into this most delicious late-night fare.

My recipe is for four individual pies that can be served as we would in Scotland on 1 January, with mash and mushy peas. Equally they would work with a thick pea soup, for a true South Australian Pie Floater.

I make the pies in little round pie tins (about 200ml capacity), measuring about 12–13cm across the top. But if you can find rectangular tins, that would make them even more authentic, as the Adelaide pies are rectangular or oval, never round.

First make the stew. Melt the butter and 1 teaspoon of oil in a wide saucepan. Toss the beef in the seasoned flour, then brown all over in the pan. Remove with a slotted spoon, then add 1 tablespoon of oil to the same pan and gently fry the onion and carrots for a few minutes. Return the meat, with the hot stock, tomato puree and Worcestershire sauce, then stir and put the heat to its lowest setting, cover and cook on the hob for 1½ – 2 hours, stirring occasionally. The time you cook the beef for depends on the heat and what cut of beef you have used. What you want is tender beef and a sauce that is nicely thick. Once done, remove, taste and adjust the seasoning, then cover and chill overnight.

To make the shortcrust pastry, put the strong and plain flours into a food processor and add the butter. Whizz briefly until it resembles breadcrumbs, then add a couple of tablespoons of cold water – just enough so that you can bring the mixture together with your hands. Cling wrap and chill for half an hour or so. You can do this by hand by rubbing in the butter, then adding enough water to bind.

Butter four 200ml-capacity baking tins (round or rectangular).

Roll out the pastry to fit the bases and sides of the baking tins.

Fill each with the cold stew.

Cut out the puff pastry to fit the tops of each tin and place on top, pressing the edges together. Pinch the edges to seal, then chill the pies again, preferably for a couple of hours.

Remove the pies to room temperature at least half an hour before baking.

Meanwhile, preheat the oven to 200°C. Place a baking tray in the oven to heat up.

Brush the top of each pie with egg, then snip a small hole in the top with scissors. Place the pies directly onto the heated baking sheet (so the shortcrust pastry begins to cook immediately) and bake in the preheated oven for 25 – 30 minutes until puffed up and golden brown.

Leave for a few minutes before decanting carefully from the tins onto warm dinner plates and serving with mashed potatoes and stir-fried cabbage or traditional mushy peas.

Or, if you are serving them as Pie Floaters, invert a pie into a shallow soup plate so that the puff side is down, shortcrust upper. Ladle in some thick pea soup (I prefer the soup around, moat-like, so the shortcrust pastry does not become soggy; it is, however, traditionally served over the top), then top with a skoosh of ketchup.

Devour with a spoon.

Smoked haddock tart

Serves 6

•

For the pastry

200g plain flour

50g parmesan, grated

150g butter, diced

1 egg, beaten

•

For the filling

400g smoked haddock fillets
(approx. 2)

200ml whole milk

100ml double cream

3 medium eggs, beaten

freshly ground black pepper

2 tbsp lovage, freshly
chopped, or 100g spinach,
wilted and patted
thoroughly dry

This is a delicious savoury tart that hardly needs any extra flavours, apart from either lovage or spinach, because the taste of smoked haddock is so sublime. It can be salty, depending on the cure, so if you can bear to taste the raw custard (milk/cream/eggs) then do so – otherwise I think it best not to add any salt; it can always be added at the table. But do add plenty of freshly ground black pepper.

Instead of two smoked haddock fillets, you can use one Finnan haddock: you may need to poach it for a little longer, but then you just flake the flesh off the bone once it's done.

In the summer, if you can find lovage (it grows in a pot in my garden) then do use this: its celery-cum-lemon flavour is perfect with the smoked fish. If not, spinach is also good but do remember to pat it dry before adding to the tart.

This is a lovely buttery pastry so I recommend placing a piece of foil on your baking sheet to avoid any buttery seepage.

For the pastry, place the flour, parmesan and butter in a food processor and whizz until it resembles breadcrumbs. Add the egg through the feeder tube and process briefly until combined.

Wrap the pastry in cling film and chill for half an hour or so.

Butter a deep, 23cm tart tin. Preheat the oven to 190°C.

Roll out the pastry to fit into the tart tin. Prick the base all over with a fork. You'll probably have a little leftover pastry: you can make 12 tiny tartlet cases to fill with a savoury filling or freeze it till you need it.

Fill the pastry case with foil and baking beans, then bake for 15–20 minutes. Remove the foil and beans, and continue to bake for a further 5 minutes or so, until just cooked. Leave to cool briefly. Lower the heat to 180°C.

Poach the haddock in the milk for 4–5 minutes until just done, then drain the fish using a sieve over a large jug or bowl, reserving the liquid

Cool the fish and the liquid, then add the cream and eggs and plenty of black pepper to the jug, mixing well.

Flake the fish into the tart case, then scatter over the lovage or spinach. Slowly pour over the custard, then place it in the oven for 30–35 minutes or until puffed up and tinged with golden brown.

Eat warm with salad.

Artichoke and Mull Cheddar tart

Mull Cheddar is one of my favourite cheeses: firm and creamy, it has a tangy and full-bodied flavour that is divine eaten as it is with good bread or oatcakes – or used in cooking in anything, from simple macaroni cheese to this delicious artichoke tart.

For the pastry, add the flour, along with the parmesan, salt and butter, to your food processor and whizz briefly until it resembles breadcrumbs. With the machine running, add the egg through the feeder tube. Process until it looks moist, adding a couple of splashes of cold water, if necessary. Gather together with your hands and wrap in cling film. Chill for about 1 hour.

Lightly butter a deep, 23cm flan tin. Roll out the pastry and line the tin, then prick the base all over with a fork. Place in the refrigerator for a couple of hours, or preferably overnight, to prevent shrinkage.

Preheat the oven to 200°C.

Bake the tart blind (lined with foil and filled with baking beans) for 15 minutes, then remove the foil and beans and return it to the oven for another 5 minutes.

Remove and cool for at least 15 minutes. Reduce the oven temperature to 190°C.

For the filling, beat together the crème fraîche, eggs, parsley and plenty of salt and pepper.

Sprinkle a tablespoon of parmesan over the pastry base, then place the well-drained artichokes on top. Top with the cheese. Pour over the crème fraiche mixture and bake for about 40 minutes until puffed up and golden brown. Cool in the tin for at least half an hour before decanting onto a serving plate.

Serves 6

•

For the pastry

200g plain flour

25g parmesan, grated

½ tsp salt

125g butter, chilled and diced

1 egg

a couple of splashes of cold water, as necessary

•

For the filling

200ml crème fraîche

3 medium eggs

2 tbsp flat leaf parsley, finely chopped

salt and freshly ground black pepper

1 tbsp parmesan, grated

1 jar of artichoke hearts in oil (290g), drained, patted dry and chopped

100g Mull Cheddar (or other good cheddar-style cheese), grated

Tomato and Stornoway black pudding tart

Serves 6 – 8

•

For the pastry

175g plain flour

25g medium oatmeal or parmesan, grated

125g butter, diced

1 egg, beaten

•

For the filling

2 tbsp parmesan, grated

1 rounded tbsp Dijon mustard or tapenade

800g (approx.) vine tomatoes, thickly sliced, patted well dry

4 – 6 slices Stornoway black pudding, skin removed, halved, or a handful of rocket

This is a very versatile tart. You can add oatmeal to the pastry for a nutty texture and taste, or parmesan for a short texture and mildly cheesy taste. You can spread the base with Dijon mustard or tapenade (olive paste – green or black). And finally, you can top it with crisp slices of black pudding or a scattering of rocket leaves.

It's really important to pat the tomato slices thoroughly dry – you'll need many sheets of kitchen paper for this.

To make the pastry, place the flour, oatmeal (or parmesan) and butter in a food processor and whizz until it resembles breadcrumbs. Add the egg while the machine is running, then stop the motor and combine in your hands. Bring together into a ball, then wrap in cling film and chill for 30 minutes or so.

Butter a shallow, 28cm tart tin. Roll out the pastry to fit, prick all over and chill again, for at least an hour or overnight.

Preheat the oven to 200°C.

Fill the pastry case with foil and baking beans and bake blind for 15 minutes, then remove the foil and beans and cook for a further 5 minutes.

Scatter the parmesan over the base while hot, then allow to cool for 20 minutes or so.

Dot over the mustard (or tapenade), then lay the tomatoes on top in tight concentric circles, so they sit proud. Season with salt and pepper, then bake in the oven for 30 minutes until tinged with golden brown. Remove from the oven.

Meanwhile, place the black pudding slices on a baking tray, put into the oven and cook for 10 – 15 minutes or until crispy.

Pat the black pudding dry with kitchen paper, then place the slices on top of the tart. Alternatively, pile the rocket into the middle of the tart for a vegetarian option.

Serve warm with salad.

Spinach, feta and mint filo rolls

These are similar to the fabulous Greek pie spanakopita, but I make mine into rolls, like sausage rolls, instead of individual or square pies. Also, instead of all spinach, I have tried it with half watercress or rocket and half spinach, which also tastes good – indeed there's a welcome bite from the peppery leaves. If you don't have fresh mint, then dill is also a good substitute, as the herb is often found in Greek spanakopita.

Serve with soup at lunch in winter, or with drinks outside in the garden in the summer. But have napkins at the ready – they are gloriously flaky.

For the filling, lightly cook the spinach until just wilted – you can do this in a microwave or in a pan with a few drops of water. If using watercress or rocket, do the same. Drain thoroughly over a colander, squeezing dry with kitchen roll and tea towels. Chop the leaves roughly, then add to a bowl with the crumbled feta, the mint (or dill) and egg. Season with salt (not too much; feta is salty) and freshly ground black pepper.

Lightly butter a large baking sheet. Preheat the oven to 200°C.

Lay out one sheet of filo, brush with butter, cover with a second sheet, brush with butter, cover with a third sheet and finish with a brushing of butter. Cut in half lengthwise, then lay some of the filling along the length, then roll the pastry over the filling to enclose, so you have two long sausage shapes. Cut each into small pieces like sausage rolls. (You can also bake the rolls whole, then cut once baked; this is usually more flaky and messy, though.)

Brush the tops with butter and place the rolls on the baking sheet. Bake in the preheated oven for about 15 minutes or until golden brown.

Serve warm.

Makes about 30

•

400g spinach

200g feta, crumbled

25g fresh mint (or dill),
leaves snipped

1 egg

salt and freshly ground
black pepper

200g (approx.)
filo pastry sheets

100g butter, melted

Corra Linn cheese and saffron filo tartlets

Makes 24

•

25g butter

1 tbsp olive oil

3 large sheets of filo pastry

150ml double cream

½ teaspoon (a good pinch) saffron threads

2 egg yolks

salt and freshly ground black pepper

75g Corra Linn (or Manchego) cheese, coarsely grated

Corra Linn is a wonderful sheep's milk cheese made by Errington's in the Borders. Often described as 'Scotland's Manchego', the Spanish hard cheese can, of course, be substituted. These are delicious served with a glass of bubbly – or dry sherry.

Lightly grease two mini-muffin tins (to make 24 tartlets). Preheat the oven to 190°C.

Melt the butter and olive oil together.

Lay out the first sheet of filo, brush with the butter and oil, top with the second, repeat the brushing, then top with the third and brush again.

Cut the filo into 24 squares. Line each cup in the muffin tin with a filo square, pressing in lightly. Don't worry about ragged edges: these add to the charm. Chill.

Meanwhile, heat the cream to just below boiling point, then add the saffron and leave to infuse for 20–30 minutes.

Bake the tartlets for 7–8 minutes until lightly browned.

For the filling, whisk the egg yolks into the cream with some salt and pepper. Fill each tartlet with some grated cheese (leaving some to scatter on top), then carefully spoon in the saffron custard. Top with the remaining cheese and bake for about 8 minutes or until the filling sets.

Serve warm.

Classic Quiche Lorraine

Quiche Lorraine has come a long way since its origins in the sixteenth century. Then it was simply a sensible way to use up local produce; bacon, cream and eggs were baked on a bread dough base (not a tart tin) rather like Provence's *pissaladière*, with its onions, anchovies and olives. Over the years the bread in the Lorraine and Provençal dishes gave way to a lighter pastry – either *pâte brisée* (shortcrust) or *pâte feuilletée* (puff pastry) – and tart tins were introduced.

Since the 1960s and '70s, when UK wine bars began serving quiche in earnest, diners have witnessed some grim, and invariably cold, offerings.

The authentic French quiche Lorraine, however, is served hot from the oven, and with nothing more than a simple salad of floppy lettuce dressed in oil, vinegar and Dijon mustard. So forget the baked potato and coleslaw, and concentrate on the classic: a crispy pastry case filled with only three ingredients – bacon, eggs and cream.

It's important to point out that the classic quiche Lorraine would never have cheese in it. But if you feel like throwing caution to the wind, scatter 50g of freshly grated cheese over just before baking. Comté or Gruyère work well – just don't expect any French person to accept it as a classic quiche Lorraine!

Make the pastry in the usual way: in a food processor, whizz the flour and butter with half a teaspooon of salt, then slowly add enough cold water to combine to a soft but not sticky ball. By hand, rub the butter into the flour and salt, then gradually incorporate the water. Wrap in cling film and chill.

Butter a shallow, 23cm metal tart tin, then roll out the pastry to fit. Prick the base all over with a fork and chill well (preferably overnight to prevent shrinkage).

Preheat the oven to 200°C.

Fill with foil and baking beans and put in the oven for 15 minutes before removing the foil and beans. Continue to cook for 5 minutes, then remove. Reduce the heat to 190°C.

Meanwhile, fry the bacon (without extra fat) in a hot frying pan until golden brown, then drain away any fat, patting dry on kitchen paper, if necessary, and cool a little. Place the bacon in the pastry base.

Beat together the cream, milk and eggs, season generously, then pour slowly over the bacon. Carefully place in the preheated oven and bake for 30–35 minutes or until golden brown. Eat warm.

Serves 6

•

For the pastry

200g plain flour,

125g butter, diced

½ tsp salt

50ml cold water

•

For the filling

200g smoked streaky bacon, diced

200ml double cream

100ml milk

3 eggs

salt and pepper, to season

Asparagus and mint tart

Serves 6–8

•

For the pastry

200g plain flour

40g parmesan, grated

pinch of salt

125g butter, diced

1 egg

•

For the filling

250g asparagus
(not too thick)

100g cheddar, grated

2 tbsp (about 15g) mint,
finely chopped

300ml double cream

3 eggs

salt and freshly ground
black pepper

I hesitate to call this a quiche, for a couple of reasons. When I was at school in the '60s, some days lunch was bacon and egg pie. And all I can recall is fatty pink bacon dotted amidst a tasteless custard with grey, hard-boiled eggs. It was not my favourite, even when I was fooled into thinking it was a different recipe when they called it bacon and egg flan . . . But no, there was just less pastry in a flan.

And then the quiche made its appearance and what travesties emerged. As I write in the Quiche Lorraine recipe (p. 161), the only three ingredients acceptable in France in an authentic quiche Lorraine are bacon, eggs and cream, cooked in a pastry base. No cheese, no herbs, no nonsense.

The wonderful grande dame of cookery writers Marguerite Patten wrote in her *Century of British Cooking* that when she demonstrated quiche Lorraine on television at the very end of the 1950s, a quiche of any description was an almost completely unknown dish in Britain.

And so began the pale imitations of that otherwise glorious classic French dish. Throughout the '60s, '70s and '80s, we all waded through worthy and hefty slabs of cold quiche, invariably made with shop-bought pastry (which was not nearly as good as it is now) and also wholemeal pastry, which gave even more of a dense, heavy feel to the resulting quiche. Exotics such as red peppers were added for colour and thrill.

The decades moved on, and with them the quiche thankfully transformed into a savoury tart; as well as the pastry being lighter, the fillings became more and more ambitious and varied. And so as the quiche nose-dived through the years, the savoury tart soared high with glorious goat's cheese and beetroot, or butternut squash and blue cheese fillings . . . until 2023.

And then a strange thing happened. In May 2023, just when we all thought we had seen the end of the quiche, a decree was issued across the land for the coronation of King Charles III. It was suggested people make a special recipe to celebrate. And when the recipe appeared, I know I was not alone in being not only disappointed but rather bemused. For it was a quiche.

The Coronation Quiche had a filling of broad beans, spinach and tarragon, which were all meant to be in season, though broad beans are seldom available in early May in Scotland. So, for a celebratory quiche/tart, I decided to use a truly seasonal vegetable instead: asparagus. And I decided against flavouring it with, to my mind, the rather too cheffy and often overpowering herb tarragon. Instead I used a rather more popular herb, mint, in a late spring tart that is worthy of any celebration. Mint should be chopped just before using in a recipe, by the way, otherwise both colour and flavour are altered.

The main thing to remember is that, in May and June, we can use local asparagus in Scotland. We have some brilliant producers in Angus and Perthshire, such as Eassie Farm in Glamis, Charleton Farm near Montrose, and Lunan Bay Farm, north of Arbroath. Out of season, you can make this with imported asparagus, obviously. There's no point in being too purist about things, but in May and June local asparagus is best. Just don't tell the King that broad beans don't appear in Scottish farm shops till July.

––––––––––

For the pastry, place the flour, parmesan, salt and butter in a food processor and whizz until it resembles breadcrumbs. Then, with the machine running, add the egg and process until it begins to clump together. Bring the dough together with your hands and wrap in cling film, then chill for half an hour or so.

Butter a shallow 28cm tart tin.

Roll out the pastry to fit the tart tin, then prick the base all over. Chill again for at least an hour, preferably overnight.

Preheat the oven to 190°C.

Break off any woody ends from the asparagus and, using the tart tin as guidance, trim the ends so the spears will fit in the base. Now steam or boil for 2–3 minutes until just tender but still bright green. Rinse under cold water to retain the colour. Pat really well dry on kitchen paper and set aside.

Fill the pastry base with foil and baking beans and bake blind in the preheated oven for 15 minutes before removing the foil and beans. Continue to bake for a further 5 minutes until just cooked through. Reduce the oven to 180°C.

While the pastry is still warm, scatter over the cheese. Once it has cooled a little, arrange the asparagus like the spokes of a wheel, with the tips pointing out around the circumference.

Mix together the mint, cream, eggs and plenty salt and pepper (I do this in my food processor). If you can bear to, taste the mixture and season as appropriate.

Pour this slowly over the asparagus (you may not need it all; perhaps a couple of tablespoons will be left over) and return the tart to the oven to bake for about 30 minutes or until puffed up and golden brown. Cool for at least half an hour, then eat warm with salad.

Partan bree tart

Partan bree is one of Scotland's traditional dishes: a rich, creamy crab soup thickened with rice. 'Partan' means crab, 'bree' means liquid or gravy. Typical in many seaside areas of Scotland, this recipe has of course many variations. Lady Clark of Tillypronie in her 1909 book suggests adding some anchovy, and so I like to finish the tart with a few of these on top.

Don't overdo the mace flavouring – a quarter teaspoon seems little but it's just enough to give that wonderful background hint without overpowering everything. Instead of using the mace and anchovies, I also add some chopped chilli to the crab filling: add 1 finely chopped red chilli to the mixture in the food processor instead of the mace, and don't top with the anchovies.

If you use a large live crab as your base for this recipe, simply boil it for 15–20 minutes, then remove the creamy brown (body) meat to one bowl and the sweet white (claw and leg) meat to another. Discard the feathery 'dead men's fingers' as you work. Otherwise, fresh or defrosted frozen crab meat will do.

This amount of pastry will give you some leftover, enough to roll out thinly, then cut into six cheesy biscuits. Prick, then bake at 180°C for about 15 minutes until pale golden. Or use as the base in tartlet cases, which you can fill with something savoury, like the quiche Lorraine mixture (see page 161).

————————

Serves 6

•

For the pastry

175g plain flour

50g parmesan, grated

125g butter, diced

pinch of salt

1 egg, beaten

•

For the filling

250g crab meat
(white and brown,
or all white)

3 eggs

¼ tsp ground mace
(or 1 red chilli, seeded
and finely chopped)

200ml crème fraîche

salt and pepper, to season

1 × tin (50g) anchovies,
drained

————————

For the pastry, place the first three ingredients in a food processor with a pinch of salt. Process briefly then, with the machine running, add the egg. You can do this by hand by rubbing the butter into the flour and parmesan until it makes breadcrumbs, then adding the egg. Bring together with your hands, then clingwrap and chill for half an hour or so.

Butter a 23cm shallow tart tin, then roll out the pastry to fit. Prick all over the base with a fork and chill well.

Preheat the oven to 200°C.

Line the pastry base with foil and fill with baking beans, then bake blind for 15 minutes. Remove the foil and beans and cook for a further 5 minutes. Take it out of the oven and cool, then reduce the temperature to 190°C.

Beat together the first four filling ingredients in a food processor, with plenty of salt and pepper (taste the raw mix if you can bear to, to ensure you have just enough seasoning). Pour the mixture into the pastry case.

Top with anchovies, if using, arranged around like spokes in a wheel, and bake for about 35 minutes or until set and tinged with golden brown.

Serve warm or cold, not hot.

Haggis tartlets with
red onion marmalade

For these delicious little canapés, you can either use the parmesan pastry in the Partan bree tart recipe opposite or use leftover savoury pastry from any of the pies or tarts you've made. Each time I have trimmings left over, I wrap them in cling film and freeze them. (Be sure to label savoury or sweet!) Then, once I have about 300g, I just defrost the pastry, roll it out and make these little tartlets.

They are delicious with a glass of bubbly and are suitable for everyone, since you can use regular or vegetarian haggis.

And, of course, there are many good commercial red onion marmalades you can use instead of making your own.

Butter 24 tartlet cases, or two mini muffin trays. Preheat the oven to 190°C.

For the pastry, once chilled, if making fresh – or defrosted, if frozen – roll out to fill the 24 tartlet cases. Prick each base lightly, then chill for an hour or so. Bake for 12–15 minutes, or until cooked through. Reheat to warm before serving.

For the marmalade, sauté the onions in the oil for 15–20 minutes until softened. Add the vinegar, wine (or cider) and sugar and increase the heat. Once bubbling, lower to a simmer, cover and cook gently for 10 minutes, then cook, uncovered, for about 20 minutes or until thick. Add seasoning to taste and cool.

To assemble, heat the haggis (either wrap in foil and place in a medium oven for about 45 minutes or until piping hot; or slit and spoon out the contents into a microwaveable bowl and cover, then microwave until hot). Slit (if heating in the oven) and spoon some into each warm pastry case. Top with a dollop of marmalade and serve at once.

Makes 24

•

300g (approx.) savoury shortcrust pastry (leftovers, or 1 batch of the parmesan pastry, see p. 166)

1 butcher's haggis

•

For the red onion marmalade

3 medium red onions, peeled, finely chopped

2 tbsp olive oil

2 tbsp red wine or cider vinegar

4 tbsp red wine (or cider)

1 tbsp dark brown sugar

freshly ground black pepper

Forfar bridies

For the pastry

250g strong white flour

50g plain flour

pinch of salt

75g butter, diced

50g dripping (or white fat), diced

2–3 tbsp cold water

•

For the filling

450g shoulder or rump beef

75g beef suet, grated

1 small onion, peeled and finely grated

salt and pepper

Bridies and pies are still very much a part of life in Dundee and Angus. And whereas the best pies have traditionally come from Dundee, the best bridies are from Forfar. J.M. Barrie mentioned bridies in one of the novels he wrote at the end of the nineteenth and early twentieth centuries. He was a native of Kirriemuir, some 5 miles north-west of Forfar, and so would have been very familiar with the bridies of Angus. According to F. Marian McNeill, the first Forfar bridie baker was a Mr Jolly in the mid nineteenth century.

My recipe is based on Bill McLaren's, whose great-grandfather James McLaren learned the skills of bridie-making at Jolly's Bakery. His family-run bakery, which opened in 1893, has baked bridies to the same recipe ever since. When I visited him some years ago, he taught me about the essential 'dunting' and 'nicking' procedure to seal the horseshoe-shaped bridie. The 'dunting' is done with the heel of the hand, pressing down on the edges. The 'nicking' is done with forefinger and thumb, to finish the sealing.

For the pastry, mix the flours and place into a food processor with a pinch of salt. Add the butter and dripping and process until incorporated. Add just enough cold water (2–3 tablespoons) to bind to a stiff dough. You can do this by hand by rubbing the butter and dripping into the flour, and adding just enough of the water to bring it together.

Gather in your hands, wrap in cling film and chill for at least 1 hour.

For the filling, roughly chop the beef – I use the pulse button on my food processor. Alternately, mince very coarsely. Mix together the beef, suet, onion and plenty of salt and pepper. The mixture should be fairly stiff.

Lightly butter a baking sheet.

Divide the pastry into four and roll each piece into an oval, the widest diameter of which is about 23cm. Divide the filling into four and spoon onto one half of each pastry oval, leaving a border all round.

Dampen the edges and fold the top half of the pastry over the filling to enclose it. Trim the edges into a neat horseshoe shape (not a half-moon: that is the Cornish pasty).

Now 'dunt and nick' – by pressing down the edges to seal and crimping all around to give a nicely finished look. Using a sharp knife, prick a small hole for steam to escape in the top of each bridie. Place on the baking tray and chill for an hour or so.

Preheat the oven to 200°C.

Bake for 30–35 minutes or until golden brown. Serve warm.

Venison bridies

Venison was often used in the past in Scotland instead of beef and lamb, as deer roamed freely before the widespread influx of sheep during and after the Highland Clearances in the eighteenth and nineteenth centuries.

There is a lovely recipe in Mrs MacIver's cookery book from 1773 for a 'Venison Pasty', which suggests adding some fat mutton to the venison if it is lean. The meat mixture is then covered with 'puff paste', which has been thickly rolled, then, once done, the instructions stipulate you 'send it to the oven; it takes a long time of baking'. Goodness knows how black the puff pastry must have been by this stage . . .

My venison bridie is rather delicious and mouth-watering. Enjoy with a glass of red and a salad.

For the pastry, place the flours and half a teaspoon of salt into a food processor. Add the butter and process until incorporated. Add just enough cold water (approx. 3 tablespoons) to bind to a stiff dough. You can do this by hand by rubbing the butter into the flour, and adding just enough of the water to bring it together.

Gather in your hands, wrap in cling film and chill for at least 1 hour.

Lightly butter a baking sheet.

For the filling, mix the venison, suet, onion and parsley, seasoning with plenty of salt and pepper.

Divide the pastry into four and roll each piece into an oval. Divide the filling into four and spoon onto one half of each pastry oval, leaving a border all round.

Dampen the edges and fold the top half of the pastry over the filling to enclose it. Trim the edges into a neat horseshoe shape. Now 'dunt' and 'nick' – by pressing down the edges to seal and crimping all around to give a nicely finished look. Using a sharp knife, prick a small hole (for steam to escape) in the top of each bridie. Place on the baking tray and chill for an hour or so.

Preheat the oven to 200°C.

Bake for 35–40 minutes or until golden brown.

Serve warm, not hot.

Makes 4

•

For the pastry

250g strong white flour

75g plain flour

½ tsp salt

175g butter, diced

3 tbsp cold water

•

For the filling

500g venison mince, coarsely minced (usually taken from the shin)

75g beef suet, grated

1 small onion, peeled and finely grated

1 rounded tbsp fresh parsley, finely chopped

salt and freshly ground black pepper

Cullen skink bridies

These wonderful bridies are ideal for non-meat eaters – made from smoked haddock and flavoured with mustard and lemon. The filling is based on that classic Scottish soup, Cullen skink, traditionally made with Finnan haddock, potatoes, onions and milk.

The bridies are delicious served warm, with a salad of chicory or watercress dressed in a good mustardy vinaigrette.

Makes 4

•

For the pastry

250g strong white flour

75g plain flour

pinch of salt

175g butter, diced

2 – 3 tbsp cold water

•

For the filling

500g undyed smoked haddock fillets

300ml whole milk

3 tbsp flat leaf parsley, plus stalks, chopped

25g butter

25g plain flour

2 rounded tsp Dijon mustard

grated zest of 1 lemon

freshly ground black pepper

For the pastry, combine the flours with a pinch of salt in a food processor. Add the butter and process until incorporated. Add just enough of the 2 – 3 tablespoons of cold water to bind to a stiff dough. You can also do this by hand by rubbing together the butter and the flour, and adding the water to bring it together.

Gather in your hands, wrap in cling film and chill for at least 1 hour.

For the filling, place the fish in a saucepan with the milk and parsley stalks. Bring slowly to the boil, bubble for 1 minute, then remove from the heat and cover. Leave for half an hour or so, then strain into a sieve placed over a jug.

Melt the butter in a saucepan, add the flour, stir for a minute, then add the reserved fish liquor and, whisking, cook over a medium-low heat until smooth. Stir in the mustard, lemon zest, chopped parsley leaves and season to taste. Cool.

Lightly butter a baking sheet.

Divide the pastry into four and roll each piece into an oval, the widest diameter of which is about 23cm. Divide the filling into four and spoon onto one half of each pastry oval, leaving a border all round.

Dampen the edges and fold the top half of the pastry over the filling to enclose it. Trim the edges into a neat horseshoe shape. Now 'dunt and nick' – by pressing down the edges to seal, and crimping all around to give a nicely finished look. Using a sharp knife, prick a small hole (for steam to escape) in the top of each bridie.

Place on the baking tray and chill for an hour or so.

Preheat the oven to 200°C.

Bake for about 40 minutes, or until a pale golden brown.

Serve warm.

Meatloaf pie

Serves 6

•

For the pastry

350g plain flour

175g butter, diced

pinch of salt

1 egg yolk

125ml soured cream

•

For the filling

1 medium onion, peeled
and finely chopped

100g mushrooms, finely
chopped (optional)

1 tbsp olive oil

1kg quality mince
(I like to use 750g beef +
250g pork mince)

grated zest of
1 medium lemon

2 rounded tbsp parsley,
finely chopped

1 egg, beaten

3 rounded tbsp parmesan,
grated

salt and freshly ground
black pepper

milk

This pie has two sources of origin.

The first goes back to when I was young and I used to adore Mrs Doig's meatloaf. Though I was always happy when asked to stay at the manse for tea, it was even better when meatloaf was on the menu! It was usually served freshly baked, hot and steaming – but it was also delicious sliced and grilled the next day. My mum's meatloaf was called meatroll, as it was made in a cylindrical pottery meatroll jar, not a rectangular baking tin.

The second source is Finland. When I lived in Kemi, my friends Ritva and Airi not only introduced me to all sorts of delicious Finnish dishes, they also made me a recipe book of the dishes I had eaten and enjoyed during my year living in northern Finland. *Lihamurekepiiras* is Finnish for meatloaf pie, a dish that is utterly delicious. Comforting and homely, it has become a great family favourite.

Ritva has her mother's cookbook from 1932 and in it there are three recipes for meatloaf. The first includes mustard; and this would be a very welcome addition to the ingredients here. The second has 'bird' or hare meat, as well as pork mince. The third has cabbage – an astonishing 1kg to only 400g of minced beef. I'm not sure this is the one for me, but the mustard and hare meatloaves I would love to try. The recipe instructions are also insistent you mince the meat twice to ensure a good texture.

In my recipe here, it is important to drain the mince once you have fried it, as mince varies in fattiness and you don't want any leakage into your short, soured cream pastry. The traditional recipe has finely chopped mushrooms in it, but you can leave these out if you have fussy no-mushroom eaters in your midst.

Also, the grated lemon is neither Finnish nor Scottish, but I love the slight tang the zest imparts to the meatloaf, especially when you use a combination of pork with beef. Lemon and pork work so well together.

In Finland, we would have eaten it with some lingonberry jam; in Scotland, I like to serve it with potatoes and green vegetables – and perhaps a spoonful of grainy mustard.

For the pastry, mix the flour and butter in a food processor with a pinch of salt until it resembles breadcrumbs. Mix the egg yolk and soured cream together, then add this through the feeder tube with the machine running. You can also do this by hand by rubbing the butter into the flour and salt, then adding the egg and soured cream mixed together.

Gather the dough into a ball, clingwrap and chill for an hour or so.

Roll out into two rectangles, about 18 × 28cm. Hang onto the trimmings: these will be used later. Wrap the rectangles and trimmings in cling film and chill for an hour or so.

For the filling, gently fry the onion (and mushrooms, if using) in the oil until softened, then add the mince, breaking it up as you stir. Cook for a further 8–10 minutes or until browned all over. Remove from the heat, then drain the liquid away over a colander.

Butter a baking tray. Preheat the oven to 190°C.

Once the meat mixture is cool, mix in a bowl with the lemon zest, parsley, beaten egg and 2 tablespoons of the parmesan. Season with salt and pepper to taste.

Place one rectangle of pastry onto the baking tray. Sprinkle the remaining parmesan cheese all over the pastry base.

Gather handfuls of the meat mixture and pat together between your palms then place along the rectangle. It looks as if it will not all fit, but I can assure you it does. Pat the mixture down into a long meatloaf shape once you have all the meat on the pastry, leaving a margin around the edges.

Place a little milk in a bowl and, using a pastry brush, brush the edges, then lay the second rectangle over the top, pressing the edges together to seal. Brush all over with some more milk.

Roll out the trimmings and cut into long strips and use these to decorate the top. You can be as artistic as you want; I just lay the strips across, diagonally. Brush again with the milk and prick all over with a fork, then place in the oven for about 45 minutes, covering loosely with foil after 20 minutes to prevent burning.

Serve warm, in slices.

Corned beef meringue pie

Serves 6

•

For the pastry

225g plain flour

125g butter, diced

pinch of salt

1 egg yolk

•

For the filling

1 tbsp olive oil

2 medium onion, peeled
and finely chopped

200g button mushrooms,
wiped clean and sliced

350g corned beef, chopped

1 tbsp Worcestershire sauce

salt and freshly ground
black pepper

2 tbsp parsley,
freshly chopped

•

For the topping

3 medium egg whites

125g mature cheddar, grated

This is a pie from my youth. It was not something my mum made; rather, when I was a waitress at the Justinlees Inn at Eskbank, the cook there, Ruby, made it for the staff regularly. I worked there in my last year of school and throughout university, during the summer holidays and sometimes the Christmas holidays, too.

Along with the older women who were waitresses all year round, I had to wear a Menzies black-and-white tartan skirt and a white top. We had to be polite to all the customers and, as a well-brought up girl, I always was. But some of the older waitresses had brilliant ripostes and put-downs for any customers who were rude or drunk. I watched and learned.

Ruby was a brilliant cook and I have lots of her recipes handwritten in my old notebook. Recipes such as 'Athenian mince', which was not unlike a moussaka but with potatoes instead of aubergines; cheese soufflé; prawn flan; and this delicious savoury pie topped with a cheesy meringue.

Ruby made her shortcrust with lard and so, if you prefer, use lard instead of the butter here. It makes a tender, almost flaky pastry.

———

For the pastry, place the flour and butter, with a pinch of salt, into a food processor and process until it resembles breadcrumbs. Add the egg yolk while the machine is running. (You can also do this by hand by rubbing the butter into the flour, then adding the egg yolk.) Bring it together into a dough with your hands. You may need to add a drop or two of water. Wrap in cling film and chill for half an hour or so.

Lightly butter a 23cm metal pie dish (about 3cm deep).

Roll out the pastry to fit the dish, prick all over with a fork and chill again, this time for at least an hour.

Preheat the oven to 190°C.

Line the pie case with foil and fill with baking beans, then bake blind for 10 minutes. Remove the foil and beans and continue to cook for a further 5 minutes or until pale and just cooked through.

Increase the temperature to 230°C.

For the filling, heat the oil in a large frying pan and fry the onions and mushrooms, stirring often, until softened, then add the corned beef and stir to break up the meat. Ruby's instructions were to 'work the sauce'. Add the Worcestershire sauce, and season with salt and pepper to taste.

Remove from the heat, then stir in the parsley. Fill the pastry case with this warm mixture.

Whisk the egg whites to stiff peaks, then fold in the cheese. Pile this on top of the filling and bake for about 10 minutes or until golden brown.

Leave for a couple of minutes before cutting and serving.

Vol-au-vents
(with prawn or mushrooms)

Makes 6

•

For the pastry

1 × packet (320g) ready-rolled
puff pastry (preferably
all butter)

1 small egg, beaten, to glaze

•

For the prawn filling

200g prawns, cooked, peeled

grated zest of 1 small lemon

juice of ½ a small lemon

3 rounded tbsp mayonnaise

1 tbsp soured cream

salt and freshly ground
black pepper

chilli flakes (optional)

My, how these take me back. In the 1960s and '70s, they were all the rage. I remember my mum reheating some ready-made vol-au-vent cases and filling them with spoonfuls of Marks & Spencer 'chunky chicken' in white sauce.

At other people's houses, you might have them with a mushroom filling (often taken from a tin of condensed mushroom soup, undiluted) or a cold prawn cocktail filling, which was basically prawns, salad cream (mayonnaise if you had it to hand; our house never did) and tomato ketchup. That was living . . . And then they disappeared.

So I decided to reinvent them, as they are so satisfactory to make from scratch – well, not actually making the puff pastry (though feel free), but with a sheet of ready-rolled puff pastry. The result? A bite of delicious nostalgia.

———

To make the vol-au-vents, first line a large baking tray with parchment paper. Lay the pastry out on a board. Using a 7.5/8cm fluted cutter, cut out 12 rounds. Flip six of them over and place on the baking parchment. Mix the egg well, then, using a pastry brush, brush all over, being very careful not to take out to the edges; if it dribbles down the side and sticks to the parchment, the pastry will not rise.

Using a 5cm cutter, cut into the remaining circles, so that you now have a small middle circle and a round circle with a hole in the middle. Place the outer circles onto the bigger circles on the tray, then carefully brush these, again being careful that the egg does not drip down the sides.

You will have six vol-au-vent-looking shapes, albeit flat. Using a fork, prick the inner base of each vol-au-vent; this inhibits the middle rising.

Brush the tops of the small circles and place those on the tray. Cover the dish and refrigerate, preferably overnight.

Next day, preheat the oven to 220°C.

Brush with egg again (the outer circle and the small circles), then bake in the oven for about 10 minutes until well risen and golden brown. Use the tip of a paring knife to cut all round the sides of the inner circle and press down gently with the butt of the knife handle, so you now have a neat cavity.

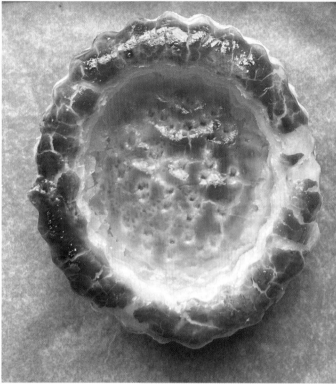

Meanwhile, prepare the fillings.

For the prawns, mix everything together, season to taste with salt and pepper, and add the chilli flakes, if using.

For the mushrooms, heat the butter in a pan and add the onions, sautéeing for a couple of minutes just until soft, then add the mushrooms and the oil. Cook until tender – about 8–10 minutes. Add the flour, stirring well. Cook for half a minute or so, then add the cream and milk, stirring well until thick. Remove from the heat and add the parmesan, then season to taste.

To serve, divide the cold prawn mixture between the warm cases. Or spoon the warm mushroom mixture into the warm cases and top with chopped chives.

For the mushroom filling

25g butter

½ small onion, peeled and finely chopped

200g chestnut mushrooms, wiped clean and finely chopped

1 tsp olive oil

25g plain flour

150ml single cream

100ml whole milk

1 tbsp parmesan, grated

1 tbsp chives, finely chopped, to garnish

Cheese straws

Makes 18–20

•

1 packet (320g) ready-rolled
all-butter puff pastry

100g Gruyère, grated

40g parmesan, grated

1 egg yolk

1 tbsp milk

Who doesn't love a cheese straw? The secret is lots of cheese and a deft hand at twisting. I like to use a combination of Gruyère and parmesan, but good old cheddar also works. You can add a pinch of cayenne pepper, if you want them spicy.

Serve warm with drinks – or with a bowl of home-made roasted tomato soup.

Line two baking trays with parchment paper. Preheat the oven to 200°C.

Unroll the pastry onto a board so that the long edge is facing you. Scatter the cheese all over the top half, leaving a very small margin around the edges. Use your fingertips to dab along the top margin with some cold water. Now flip the nearest edge over to meet the top edge, encasing all the cheese. Press the edges together to seal.

Using a rolling pin, roll out a little in both directions, but gently, so you don't tear the pastry. You want it just a little longer and wider, but still in a rectangle.

With a sharp knife, cut the pastry into about 20 × 1cm-wide long strips. Hold each end of the strip, one with each hand, and twist, giving it 4–5 turns; do this with a quick and deft movement so you don't lose the cheese. Also, it's best to twist the straw above the rest of the pastry, so any bits of cheese that escape fall over the remaining pastry.

Place these on the baking tray, spacing them apart and pressing their ends down so they don't unfurl while they bake.

Mix the egg yolk and milk and, using a pastry brush, paint the tops lightly with this mixture, trying not to press down and spoil the beautiful twisted shape.

Bake in the oven for about 15 minutes or until golden brown. Swap the trays around if you are using one oven for both trays. Remove them to a wire rack and eat warm, preferably with a nice glass of something fizzy.

Westray Wife and
caramelised red onion quiche

Westray Wife is an exquisite organic cheese from the Orkney island of Westray. Made by Jason and Nina Wilson, from their small herd of Ayrshire cows, the washed-rind cheese tastes delicately nutty and almost grassy, with a wonderfully yielding yet firm texture. Raclette is a good substitute cheese for this quiche.

The cheese is named after a small Neolithic figurine about 5,000 years old, found in an archaeological dig on the Links of Noltland, beside the Wilsons' farm. It is the earliest human carving found in Scotland.

Their farm is a mere 20-minute stroll from the Pierowall Hotel in the main village on Westray and the cheese is made into this delicious quiche by hotel owner Mabel Kent, whose legendary cooking brings diners from all over the islands and mainland Scotland.

For the pastry, put the flour and butter into a food processor and whizz until it resembles breadcrumbs. With the machine running, add about 50ml of cold water – or just enough for the mixture to begin to clump. With your hands, bring the dough together and wrap in cling film. Chill for half an hour or so in the fridge.

Butter a shallow 25cm tart tin and roll out the pastry to fit. Prick the base all over. Chill for at least a couple of hours.

Preheat the oven to 190°C.

Line the tart base with foil and fill with baking beans, then blind bake for 15 minutes. Remove the foil and beans and continue to bake for a further 5 minutes. Leave to cool.

Reduce the oven temperature to 180°C.

Gently fry the sliced onion in olive oil, stirring for about 15 – 20 minutes, then add the sugar and vinegar. Stirring continuously, let it bubble away until thick, then allow it to cool a little.

Spread this carefully over the tart case, then scatter the cheese evenly over the top. Mix the eggs, cream and plenty salt and ground pepper, then slowly pour this over the filling. Bake in the oven for 35 – 40 minutes or until puffed up and golden brown.

Serves 6 – 8

•

For the pastry

225g plain flour

150g butter, diced

50ml (approx.) cold water

•

For the filling

1 large red onion
(or 2 medium), peeled
and thinly sliced

1 tbsp olive oil

1 rounded tbsp soft
brown sugar

1 tbsp balsamic vinegar

125g Westray Wife cheese,
grated (or Raclette, thinly
sliced)

4 eggs

200ml double cream

salt and freshly ground
black pepper

Hot smoked salmon
and watercress tart

————————

This is a taste of summer, not only because of its fresh flavours but also the beautiful pink and green colours. Serve with a simple salad and either good bread or new potatoes, tossed in butter.

   If you can't find watercress, you can use rocket instead.

————————

For the pastry, place the flour and butter in a food processor with a pinch of salt. Process briefly, then, with the machine running, add the egg. Bring together with your hands, then clingwrap and chill for half an hour or so.

Butter a deep, 23cm tart tin.

Roll out the pastry to fit the tin, prick all over with a fork and chill well, preferably overnight.

Preheat the oven to 190°C.

Line the pastry base with foil and fill with baking beans and bake blind for 15 minutes, then remove the foil and beans and cook for a further 5–10 minutes until just cooked. Remove from the oven.

Sprinkle the parmesan over the base while it's still hot. Then cool.

Reduce the oven to 180°C.

Scatter the salmon and watercress over the base, pressing down a little.

Whisk together the eggs, lemon zest and crème fraîche, seasoning with salt and pepper, then slowly pour over the filling.

Bake for 30–40 minutes until set and tinged with golden brown.

Serve warm or cold with salad.

Serves 4–6

•

For the pastry

200g plain flour

125g butter, diced

pinch of salt

1 egg, beaten

•

For the filling

2 rounded tbsp parmesan, grated

300g hot-smoked salmon, flaked

50g watercress, coarse stalks removed, roughly chopped

3 eggs

grated zest of 1 lemon

200ml crème fraîche

salt and freshly ground black pepper

7
Sweet pies & tarts

Introduction

As well as a 'plate' rhubarb or apple tart, my mum used to make Border tarts, and when I discovered their many variations (Ecclefechan, Eyemouth, Melrose) I was overjoyed, for if there's one thing I love it's a Border tart.

Sweet things encased in pastry go back a long way. I'm lucky to have facsimile reproductions of a couple of old recipe books – and have been fortunate enough to see the originals in the National Library of Scotland and the Innerpeffray Library.

Mrs MacIver's curd tartlets are from her recipe book originally written in 1773 and on display at Innerpeffray. They are not only delicious but also rather international in flavour. The florentine curd tartlets in her book, simply entitled 'A Curd Florentine', with its sweet curd and spinach filling, are not dissimilar to Italian sweet spinach pies, specialities dating back to the Middle Ages in Tuscany.

A sweet pie is a delight, and if it's too warm to accompany with the customary jug of custard, then opt for ice cream, or, if you're Scottish, both.

Previous page: Linzertorte (aka Posh jam tart), p. 198
Below: Border tart, p. 204

Deep apple pie

This not only tastes divine, it looks rather fabulous. It is a seriously deep apple pie based on a Dutch recipe, where cinnamon is used generously. It is an optional extra in this recipe, and sometimes I prefer to leave it out so that the lemon flavour can also sing.

Serve with custard or ice cream – or both.

For the pastry, place the flour, sugar and butter in a food processor and whizz until combined, then add the egg while the machine is running and process. Bind together with your hands, wrap in cling film and chill in the fridge for 30 – 45 minutes.

Meanwhile, lay the apple slices out on a couple of large trays lined with kitchen paper. Leave for a minimum of 30 minutes (or up to a couple of hours): they will go brown, but don't panic. This dries them out and intensifies the flavour.

Butter a deep, 20cm springform cake tin. Preheat the oven to 180°C.

Roll out the pastry and use two-thirds to line your tin. Roll out the rest for the lid.

Put the sugar, cinnamon (if using), lemon zest and flour in a bowl and mix. Tip the apples into the bowl, then mix everything thoroughly. Place the apples in the pastry-lined tin, squashing them down with your hands. Don't worry – they will all go in, it might just look a little bulgy!

Dampen the edges of the pastry in the tin with water. Top with the pastry lid and press the edges together, trimming off any extra pastry. Using your forefingers and thumbs, crimp around the edges for a neat finish.

Whisk the egg yolk lightly with a fork, then, using a pastry brush, brush over the top of the pie. Sprinkle over a little caster sugar (a teaspoon or so is fine) and make two slits in the lid.

Place in the preheated oven for about an hour, covering loosely with foil after half an hour or so to prevent the top burning. Leave for 30 minutes or so before removing carefully from the tin and serving warm or cold.

Serves 8

•

For the pastry

300g plain flour

25g caster sugar

175g butter, diced

1 egg

•

For the filling and glaze

2kg cooking apples, cored and sliced

200g caster sugar

1 tsp ground cinnamon (optional)

grated zest of 1 lemon

2 tbsp plain flour

1 small egg yolk

caster sugar

Eighteenth-century curd tartlets

There are several well-known recipes for currant curd tarts and cheesecakes from the eighteenth century, including those by John Farley in his *The London Art of Cookery* (1789). I found the basis for my recipe in an even older book at Innerpeffray, Scotland's oldest free public lending library, established in 1680, in rural Perthshire. The library has produced a facsimile edition of Mrs MacIver's wonderful *Cookery and Pastry* (first published in 1773 in Edinburgh; the facsimile is from the 1789 edition).

The main recipe is for 'Curd-cheese Cakes', but there is also a recipe for a 'Curd Florentine' in the book, which has the same currant filling but with the addition of spinach and orange flower water instead of cinnamon and orange zest. Both are utterly delicious.

The Keeper of Books at Innerpeffray, Lara Haggerty, told me that in the late eighteenth century currants would have been imported into Edinburgh from Italy and raisins were from Spain.

In both recipes, you have to first make the curd by separating it from the whey. Then the curd is beaten in a mortar and mixed with the flavourings: for the curd-cheese cake these are sugar, eggs, currants, cinnamon and orange zest. For the curd florentine, it is sweet almonds, rose or orange flower water, currants and 'sweetened' spinach.

Both recipes give instructions for the pastry: to lay 'fine puff'd paste' into a dish for the florentine recipe, and into several patty pans for the cheesecake one. The filling is spooned in, then they are topped with a lattice of remaining pastry. The final instruction is to 'put them in the oven, and fire them'. Hopefully my instructions are easy enough to follow, as I have given specific oven temperatures and timings, something unknown to cooks centuries ago.

First roll out the pastry as thinly as possible (even if you have bought ready-rolled pastry, roll it out a little more).

Butter two shallow tartlet or mini muffin tins, whose 12 indentations each measure about 6.5cm across the top. You won't use all 24.

Using a 6.5cm fluted cutter, cut out 15 rounds of the pastry and press into the holes. Prick the base of each and chill for half an hour or so.

Preheat the oven to 200°C.

Makes 15–16

•

200g all-butter puff pastry

275g curd cheese

100g caster sugar

3 medium eggs

75g currants

•

For the curd-cheese cakes

½ tsp ground cinnamon

grated zest of
1 medium orange

•

For the curd florentine

50g young spinach,
cooked, patted thoroughly dry,
chopped

1 tbsp orange flower water

Blind bake the tartlet cases (without using foil and baking beans) for about 5–8 minutes or until the pastry has begun to rise. Remove from the oven and, using a teaspoon, gently push the pastry back down to line the holes again.

For the filling, beat the curd cheese, sugar and eggs together, then stir in the currants.

For the curd-cheese cakes, add the cinnamon and orange zest, stirring well. For the curd florentine (having ensured the spinach is patted thoroughly dry), add the spinach and orange flower water to the mix, stirring well.

Spoon the filling between each of the pastry cases, then return to the oven to bake for 18–20 minutes or until the curd is set, lightly tinged with golden brown, and the pastry is cooked through.

Shetland rhubarb tart

I stayed at the wonderful Burrastow House on the west coast of Shetland's Mainland many years ago when the talented Bo Simmons was cooking. Her dinners were legendary. When I returned recently, I was certainly not disappointed with the food; indeed, it was just as good.

A highlight was the rhubarb tart for dessert. It was so light yet creamy, I was blown away. Pierre Dupont, chef-owner of Burrastow House since 2005, kindly gave me his recipe and I have based the following one on this.

It is important to slice the rhubarb really thinly, as it's not in the oven long.

You don't need any cream served with this – the custard filling is creamy enough.

For the pastry, place the flour, butter and sugar in a food processor. Whizz briefly, then add 1 – 1½ tablespoons of cold water: just enough for the dough to come together into clumps.

Butter a 20cm tart tin.

Bring the dough together with your hands and place in the tin. Using the palms of your hands, spread the pastry out to fill the tart tin (base and sides) evenly. It is a thin pastry.

Prick the base with a fork and chill for a couple of hours.

Preheat the oven to 180°C.

Place the tart case in the oven (without foil and beans) for 12 minutes, then remove.

Chop, then slice the rhubarb as thinly as possible.

Place the eggs, caster sugar and cream in a bowl and, using a balloon whisk, whisk together until thick.

Distribute the rhubarb evenly in the tart case, then slowly pour over the custard. Bake in the oven for about 20 – 25 minutes until it is just set; there should still be a gently wobble in the centre.

Remove and cool before cutting into slices

Serves 6

·

For the pastry

150g plain flour

75g butter, diced

1 tbsp caster sugar

1 – 1½ tbsp cold water

·

For the filling

300 – 325g rhubarb, preferably pink and tender, trimmed

2 eggs

100g caster sugar

100ml double cream

Pecan pie

Serves 8
(or makes 24 tassies)

·

For the pastry

150g plain flour

50g ground roasted hazelnuts
(or ground almonds)

25g caster sugar

100g butter, diced

1 egg

·

For the filling

100g butter

100g light muscovado sugar

3 tbsp golden syrup

grated zest and juice of
1 large lemon

3 eggs

300g pecans, roughly chopped

2 tbsp quince jelly
(optional)

This can be made as a large tart or 24 individual little ones, also known as tassies. 'Tassie' is used in the southern states of the US to mean little tartlets, but it's also a Scots word meaning a cup or drinking goblet, from the French *la tasse*. The Auld Alliance brought us so many words, some still in use, such as *gigot* for leg of lamb and *ashet* for platter.

Robert Burns wrote a wonderful poem called 'The Silver Tassie', which starts: 'Go bring to me a pint of wine / And fill it in a silver tassie'. Well, that sounds rather nice . . .

But, back to our pie. I sometimes brush it, once out of the oven, with a glaze of melted quince jelly to give it a lovely sheen. I make jelly from the japonica in our garden, but real quince, with their gloriously fragrant smell and taste, is best if you can get your hands on them. And to over-egg the pudding, serve with some quince cream, made by stirring a tablespoon of quince eau de vie into a 250g tub of mascarpone: the result is divine.

It can also be made with walnuts, if you can't find pecans, or just for a change.

———

For the pastry, place the flour, ground nuts and sugar in a food processor and add the butter. Process until it resembles breadcrumbs, then add the egg through the feeder tube and process briefly until combined. Bring together with your hands, then wrap in cling film and chill for at least 30 minutes.

Butter a deep 23cm tart tin.

Roll out the pastry to fit the tin or, if making tassies, roll out and cut with a small cutter, then fit into 24 little tartlet tins.

Prick the base with a fork and chill for a couple of hours.

Preheat the oven to 200°C.

Fill the large pie with foil and baking beans. For the little ones, place a small piece of foil and a couple of baking beans in each. Blind bake for 15 minutes for the big tart, and 10 for the tassies, then remove the foil and beans and continue to bake for a further 5 minutes (2–3 minutes will do for the tassies). Remove from the oven.

Reduce the oven to 180°C.

For the filling, melt the butter, then beat in the sugar, syrup, and zest and juice of the lemon, then beat in the eggs one at a time. Stir in the nuts, then use this to fill the pie; if you are making the tassies, you may have some filling left over.

Bake for about 25 – 30 minutes for the pie, and 15 – 20 minutes for the tassies.

If you are using the quince jelly glaze, melt the jelly with a couple of drops of water (depending on the thickness of the jelly), then brush over the tart using a pastry brush.

Serve warm.

Treacle tart

Treacle tart was not part of my mum's repertoire. When I encountered it at school dinners, however, with my well-developed Scottish sweet tooth, I, of course, enjoyed it, with loads of lumpy school custard over it. But if you think about it – the classic recipe is, well, rather odd. Breadcrumbs and golden syrup baked in a pie: how could that possibly taste anything other than overly sweet?

Over the years, I have tasted many divine treacle tarts, without the cloying taste and texture that can come from an abundance of golden syrup. One of the best is at Ondine, Roy Brett's wonderful Edinburgh restaurant. So when I saw that he added some ground almonds to the filling, I tried a little – and liked the texture far more than those school dinner offerings. So that – and the lemon and the cream, of course – also helped. I also like to add a little black treacle to enhance both colour and rich flavour.

Serve warm with good old-fashioned custard – or clotted cream.

For the pastry, place the flour, almonds, sugar and butter in a food processor and whizz until it resembles breadcrumbs. Add the egg through the feeder tube. Gather the mixture with your hands to form a dough, then wrap it in cling film and chill for about an hour.

Butter a deep 23cm tart tin.

Roll out to fit the tin, prick all over and chill for a couple of hours – or overnight.

Preheat the oven to 200°C.

Fill the pastry case with foil and baking beans and bake blind for 15 minutes, then remove the foil and beans and cook for a further 5 minutes. Leave to cool slightly. Reduce the temperature to 170°C.

Gently warm the syrup and treacle together (in a pan or a microwave), then add the breadcrumbs, almonds and grated lemon zest and juice. Beat everything together, then add the eggs, stirring well. Finally, stir in the cream.

Tip into the pastry case and bake for about 25–30 minutes, or until there is still a slight wobble in the centre. Leave to become completely cold before serving.

Serves 8

•

For the pastry

175g plain flour

25g ground almonds

25g caster sugar

100g butter, diced

1 egg

•

For the filling

6 rounded tbsp golden syrup

1 rounded tbsp black treacle

100g fresh white breadcrumbs

50g ground almonds

grated zest and juice of
1 large lemon

2 eggs, beaten

200ml double cream

Mincemeat and apple slice, with polenta crumble topping

Makes 12–16 slices

•

225g sweet shortcrust pastry

400g quality mincemeat

2 large cooking apples, peeled, cored and grated

1 tbsp polenta

•

For the crumble

75g self-raising flour

50g polenta

75g butter, diced

50g demerara sugar

1 tsp ground cinnamon

These delicious little squares are part mince pie, part apple pie, part crumble – what better combination? I usually keep any leftover pastry, sweet or savoury, and clingwrap and freeze it. So when I have a few balls of leftover sweet pastry, I make something like this. You will need about 225g of sweet shortcrust (or you can make it from scratch, following the instructions in the Pecan pie or Treacle tart recipes).

Butter a shallow 18 × 28cm baking tin.

Roll out the pastry thinly, then line the tin. Prick all over with a fork. Chill well.

Preheat the oven to 200°C.

Mix the mincemeat and grated apple. Sprinkle the tablespoon of polenta over the pastry, then tip the apple mixture over the base, smoothing out the top.

For the crumble, combine the flour and polenta, then rub in the butter until it resembles breadcrumbs. Stir in the sugar and cinnamon and, once combined, tip this over the mixture in the tin. Press down gently with your hands, then bake for about 25–30 minutes or until golden brown.

Remove and cool before cutting into squares.

Rhubarb plate pie

Rather like the mince round, this is another 'plate' pie well-loved throughout Scotland. In Dundee, it is always called a tart, even though the distinction elsewhere between tart and pie is often that a tart has no pastry lid. For my parents, it was always apple or rhubarb tart, baked on a shallow enamel plate, pastry underneath and as a lid. Unless, of course, you went to a baker's and bought some dinky little rhubarb pies (no one made these at home) – shaped like a Scotch pie but sweet and oozing with pink syrupy juices.

Though not traditional, you can add some finely chopped stem ginger (1–2 balls) from a jar of ginger in syrup.

For the pastry, combine the flours, butter and icing sugar in a food processor, then, with the machine running, add the egg and process until the mixture is a little clumpy. Combine with your hands, wrap in cling film, then chill for an hour or so.

Butter a 23cm enamel pie plate.

Roll out half the pastry to fit the plate.

For the filling, combine everything together, then tip into the pie. It will seem like a lot of filling, but it will all go in. You want a nice mound.

Roll out the remaining pastry, dampen the edges, then use it to cover the fruit before pinching the edges neatly together.

Preheat the oven to 200°C.

Glaze by brushing all over with the egg yolk, then sprinkle with sugar on top. Using scissors, snip a little hole in the middle. Chill for 10–15 minutes until the egg sets.

Bake for 10 minutes, then reduce the temperature to 190°C and continue to bake for a further 25–30 minutes (so 35–40 minutes in all), covering loosely with foil after the first 15 minutes to prevent the pastry burning.

Test it is ready by poking through the hole with a metal skewer to check the rhubarb is tender.

Serve warm, not hot, with thick cream or custard.

Serves 8

•

For the pastry

150g self-raising flour

100g plain flour

150g butter, diced

50g icing sugar

1 egg

•

For the filling

500g rhubarb (preferably young and pink), trimmed and chopped

2 tbsp plain flour

100g light muscovado sugar

1–2 balls stem ginger, chopped (optional)

•

For the glaze

1 egg yolk

caster sugar

Rhubarb and white chocolate lattice pie

Serves 8

•

For the pastry

225g plain flour

25g caster sugar

125g butter, diced

pinch of salt

1 egg, beaten

•

For the filling

700g rhubarb, trimmed
and chopped

50g caster sugar

2 tbsp water

100g best quality white
chocolate, coarsely grated,
or finely chopped chips

•

For the glaze

1 tbsp double cream (or milk)

2 tsp caster sugar

This is a rather fancier version of a plate rhubarb tart, with the sweetness of the white chocolate perfectly balancing the inherent tartness of the fruit. Try to use early season rhubarb, both to avoid the stringiness of older rhubarb and also to hopefully have a tender pink – not green – colour.

Don't be put off making a lattice: the correct way to do it is to place half the strips over the tart, then fold back every other one halfway. Place one of the remaining strips across the unfolded strips at one end, before unfolding the folded strips. Then fold back the alternative strips and continue, so they go under and over the strips until the lattice is finished.

If you think life is too short to make a proper lattice, however, there are two alternatives: buy a lattice pie crust cutter, or cheat. The latter is done by placing one strip across the top edge of the tart, then another at right angles over the first strip. Continue until they are all used up, starting with alternative sides of the tart each time. It's not authentically woven, but still looks pretty good.

Serve the tart warm with thick yoghurt or lightly whipped cream.

———

Butter a deep (preferably fluted) 23cm loose-based tart tin.

First make the pastry by placing the flour, sugar, butter and a pinch of salt in a food processor and whizzing until it resembles breadcrumbs. Add the egg through the feeder tube while the machine is running, then gather the dough together in your hands. You may need a splash of cold water if it does not come together into a ball. Wrap in cling film and chill for an hour or so.

Roll out two-thirds of the pastry and use it to line the tin. Prick the base all over with a fork. Roll out the remaining pastry to form a rectangle approx. 28 × 20cm. Cut this into 8 – 10 strips. Place these on a board, cover tightly with cling film and chill, with the lined tin, for a couple of hours, or overnight.

Preheat the oven to 190°C.

Line the pastry with foil and fill with baking beans, then bake blind for 10 – 12 minutes. Remove the foil and beans and continue to bake for a further 5 – 6 minutes until it is just cooked but still pale.

For the filling, place the rhubarb and sugar with 2 tablespoons of water in a saucepan and bring slowly to the boil, stirring till the sugar is dissolved. Cook for about 5–10 minutes or until the rhubarb is just tender. Drain in a sieve over a small pan. Boil up these juices until you have a couple of tablespoons of the liquid left.

Sprinkle the white chocolate over the pastry base, then spoon over the rhubarb. Drizzle 1 tablespoon of the rhubarb juices all over.

Remove the pastry strips from the fridge and place these over the tart to form the lattice. Trim any ragged edges. Using a pastry brush, brush the cream (or milk) over the pastry strips carefully, then sprinkle over the caster sugar.

Bake in the preheated oven for about 30 minutes or until the pastry is golden brown. Allow the tart to sit for at least half an hour before decanting and serving warm.

Linzertorte (aka Posh jam tart)

Serves 8

•

125g roasted hazelnuts, chopped

125g plain flour

50g caster sugar

¼ tsp ground cinnamon

125g butter, chilled, diced

grated zest of 1 large lemon

1 egg yolk

juice of ½ large lemon

300g best quality raspberry jam, preferably home-made

icing sugar, to dust

Sachertorte and Linzertorte are probably the best-known Austrian tortes. Sachertorte is a rich chocolate cake filled with apricot jam. Linzertorte is really the ultimate jam tart: a rich nutty pastry filled with best quality raspberry jam.

I used this recipe when I did a cookery demonstration at the Royal Highland Show some years ago. Even though it was late June, the weather was not kind: I had to become used to the noise of rain battering down on the canvas and the marquee flapping noisily in the chill wind.

Some years after that, I was demonstrating the same recipe at the Folklife Festival at the Smithsonian Institute in Washington DC in early July. The contrast in weather could not have been greater: in Washington it was 38°C most days and the tent was like an oven even before I had to switch mine on.

Both Linzertortes seemed to go down well with the crowds, however, so that was surely the most important thing.

Serve warm for pudding with some thick cream and fresh raspberries, or cold with a cup of coffee.

Blitz the hazelnuts in a food processor until finely ground, then add the flour, sugar and cinnamon. Add the butter and process until it resembles breadcrumbs.

Add the lemon zest, then process very briefly before adding the egg yolk and lemon juice. Process until a dough is formed. Chill for at least 1 hour.

Meanwhile, butter a fluted 20cm flan/tart tin and sprinkle some flour inside (the easiest way to do this is with a flour shaker).

Roll out two-thirds of the pastry and line the tin. Prick the base all over with a fork. Chill for at least 20 minutes.

Preheat the oven to 180°C and place a baking sheet on the shelf.

Evenly spread the jam over the pastry base.

Roll out the remaining pastry and arrange, in lattice strips, over the top (see the introduction to the Rhubarb white chocolate lattice tart or just place alternate strips over the top).

Bake on the baking sheet (the sheet helps bake the base, since it is not blind-baked) for 35–40 minutes, until the pastry is crisp and golden.

Dust while still warm with the sifted icing sugar.

Cinnamon nablab

Makes about 20 squares

•

For the pastry

350g sweet shortcrust pastry (use the recipe from Paradise slice, p. 203)

•

For the filling

200g currants

4 tbsp water

75g light muscovado sugar

1 rounded tsp ground cinnamon

2 tbsp cornflour, slaked in 2 tbsp water

•

For the cake

225g butter, softened

225g caster sugar

4 medium eggs

225g self-raising flour

1 tsp ground cinnamon

•

For the icing

200g icing sugar, sifted

2 rounded tsp ground cinnamon

2 tbsp (approx.) water

The But'n'Ben at Auchmithie, near Arbroath, is home to some of the finest traditional home-cooking. Margaret Horn was in charge in the kitchen for many years and then – as now – only the best local produce, such as marvellous fresh shellfish and fish, especially Arbroath smokies, is found. Everything is home-made, from the jam to spread on the towering scones to the soups, puddings and cakes.

One of my favourites from the magnificent cake trolley is cinnamon nablab: a pastry base with a currant filling, spiced sponge topping, then cinnamon-flavoured icing. This is a speciality which Margaret, who was born and bred in the tiny hamlet of Auchmithie, remembers from her childhood. Nablabs have been around for many years in Arbroath. To supplement the nablabs the Auchmithie villagers made themselves at home, there were regular deliveries in bakers' vans from nearby Arbroath.

In the bakers' shops in Arbroath, there have traditionally been three types of nablab: one iced with brown (cinnamon) icing; another with white icing; and a very special pink-iced nablab, which used to have sixpences wrapped up in the cake mix. Although both white- and brown-iced nablabs have a currant filling, the pink-iced one usually has a jam filling, making it reminiscent of a bakewell pudding or tart.

Nowadays, Keptie bakery in Arbroath sells two different types of nablab, one with jam instead of the currant filling, the other with lemon curd. Both are delicious.

The etymology of nablab is interesting: in north-eastern Scots dialect, nab (sometimes written 'knab') means a morsel of food, or a bite. Lab ('leb' or 'laib') means to lick or gobble up. Perhaps nablabs were, after the famous smokie, Arbroath's second 'fast food'.

Although Margaret has always made her cinnamon nablab in a round 25cm-deep tin, my adaptation of her recipe here fits a swiss-roll tin.

———————

Lightly butter a swiss-roll tin (23 × 33cm).

Roll out the pastry and line the tin with it. Prick all over with a fork. If time permits, leave in the fridge overnight. If not, leave for at least 2 hours.

For the filling, place the currants and water in a small saucepan. Bring slowly to the boil, then stir in the sugar and cinnamon. Reduce the heat slightly and add the slaked cornflour, then, stirring constantly, bring to the boil. Cook for a couple of minutes until thickened. Allow to cool for a least 10 minutes.

Preheat the oven to 200°C.

For the cake, place the butter in a food mixer. Beat well until really soft, then add the sugar and beat well until creamy and light. Add the eggs, one at a time, beating well after each addition, adding a spoonful of the flour after the second egg. Then fold in the remaining flour and cinnamon.

Spread the currant filling over the pastry base, then top with the cake mix, spreading it well out to cover the filling completely. Place in the preheated oven for about 30 – 40 minutes, until it is well risen and cooked through: a wooden cocktail stick, inserted in the middle, should come out clean. Cover with foil for the last 10 minutes or so, to prevent burning. Leave to cool completely.

Cut into four large sections and carefully decant these (with a fish slice) onto a wire rack. (This makes it easier to decant.) Beat all the icing ingredients together, then spread over the cooled cake. Leave the icing to set, then cut into smaller squares – about 20 altogether.

Paradise slice

This is another great childhood favourite of mine. Pastry, jam and a fruit-studded coconut cake mixture on top . . . Paradise indeed!

For the pastry, place the flour, almonds and sugar in a food processor. Combine briefly, then add the butter and whizz until it resembles breadcrumbs. Slowly add the egg through the feeder tube, stopping the machine the minute it starts to form into clumps. Clingwrap and chill for a half hour or so.

Lightly butter a swiss-roll tin (23 × 33cm).

Roll the pastry out and fit inside the buttered tin. Prick all over and chill for a couple of hours, or overnight.

Preheat the oven to 200°C.

Line the pastry with foil and fill it with baking beans. Blind bake for about 15 minutes, then remove the foil and beans, and cook for a further couple of minutes until just cooked but before the edges brown. Remove and cool briefly.

Spread with the jam.

Lower the oven to 180°C.

Place the sugar, almonds and coconut in a food processor, whizz briefly, then add the butter. Process until combined, then add the eggs and rice flour. Process briefly again, then remove the mixture from the processor to a bowl and stir in the dried fruit. Spoon this carefully over the jam, smoothing the surface.

Bake for about 40–45 minutes, or until golden brown and set, covering loosely with foil after half an hour, if it's browning too quickly.

Remove to a wire rack and cool completely before cutting into slices.

Makes about 20

•

For the pastry

250g plain flour

50g ground almonds

25g caster sugar

150g butter, diced

1 egg, beaten

•

6 tbsp (approx.) home-made raspberry jam

250g caster sugar

75g ground almonds

75g desiccated coconut

200g butter, softened

2 eggs

150g rice flour (also called ground rice)

250g sultanas

100g glacé cherries, halved

Border tart

For the pastry

150g plain flour

50g ground almonds

125g butter, diced

25g caster sugar

pinch of salt

1 egg, beaten

·

For the filling

100g butter, softened

100g dark muscovado sugar

2 eggs, beaten

400g raisins

grated zest of 1 large lemon

1 tsp mixed spice

This is based on one of my mother's teatime specials. These days, border tart is a shortcrust pastry case filled with a rich, spiced raisin filling, to which I add the grated zest of a lemon. Originally it was an enriched yeasted pastry case filled with almonds, raisins, peel and marzipan, all bound together in an egg custard. The dough for the base would have been a portion taken from the weekly bread-making.

There are similar tarts to be found all over the Borders, most noticeably Eyemouth tart, which is similar, with raisins and brown sugar in the filling, but the Eyemouth version also has coconut, walnuts and glacé cherries. Ecclefechan tart is similar, too, but without the cherries and coconut. And finally there is a Melrose tart, a ginger sponge baked in pastry.

To make the pastry, place the flour, almonds, butter and sugar in a food processor with a pinch of salt. Process until it resembles breadcrumbs, then add the egg and process briefly until it begins to clump together. Bring the mixture together with your hands, wrap in cling film and chill for 1 hour.

Butter a shallow 23cm tart tin.

Roll out the pastry to fit, then prick the base all over and chill for at least 2 hours, preferably overnight.

Preheat the oven to 200°C.

Line the pastry case with foil and fill with baking beans, then bake for 10 minutes. Remove the foil and beans at this stage and continue to bake for 5 minutes more, before removing from the oven.

Reduce the temperature to 180°C.

For the filling, beat together the butter and sugar, then stir in the eggs, raisins, lemon zest and spice. Tip this into the part-baked pastry case and bake for about 30 minutes until set. Cover the tin loosely with foil for the last 10 minutes or so, to prevent the raisins burning.

Allow the tart to cool and serve in slices with tea or coffee.

Eyemouth tart

Eyemouth is a fishing town on the south-east coast of Scotland, famous for its wonderful seafood – and its tarts!

Butter a shallow 23cm tart tin. Roll out the pastry to fit, then prick the base all over and chill for at least 2 hours, preferably overnight.

When you are ready to bake, preheat the oven to 200°C.

Line the pastry case with foil and baking beans and bake for 10 minutes before removing the foil and beans. Continue to bake for 5 minutes more, then remove from the oven. Reduce the temperature to 180°C.

For the filling, beat together the butter and sugar, then stir in the remaining ingredients. Tip into the pastry case and bake for about 30 minutes or until set, covering loosely with foil for the last 10 minutes or so to prevent the raisins burning.

Serves 8

•

For the pastry

Use the Border tart sweet pastry ingredients and method (p. 204)

•

For the filling

100g butter, softened

100g dark muscovado sugar

2 eggs, beaten

250g raisins

75g desiccated coconut

75g walnuts, chopped

25g glacé cherries, halved

Ecclefechan tart

A variation of the classic Border tart, this is from Ecclefechan, a town to the south-west of the Borders. This tart has the addition of walnuts and cinnamon. You can substitute pecans for the walnuts and, indeed, to my mind, an Ecclefechan is better than America's pecan pie.

Serve this cold with tea – or barely warm, with a dollop of whipped cream and perhaps a scattering of chopped toasted walnuts on top for pudding.

Butter a shallow 23cm tart tin. Roll out the pastry to fit the tin, then prick the base all over and chill for at least 2 hours, preferably overnight.

Preheat the oven to 200°C.

Line the pastry case with foil and baking beans, and bake for 10 minutes, then remove the foil and beans and continue to bake for 5 minutes more before removing from the oven. Reduce the temperature to 180°C.

For the filling, beat together the butter and sugar, then stir in the eggs, raisins, lemon zest and juice, the nuts and cinnamon. Tip into the pastry case and bake for about 25 – 30 minutes or until set, covering loosely with foil for the last 10 minutes or so to prevent the raisins burning.

Allow the tart to cool, then serve cold with a cup of tea – or warm for pudding with cream and toasted nuts.

Serves 8

•

For the pastry

Use the Border tart sweet pastry ingredients and method (p. 204)

•

For the filling

100g butter, softened

100g dark muscovado sugar

2 eggs, beaten

250g raisins

grated zest of 1 large lemon, plus 1 tbsp lemon juice

100g walnuts, chopped

½ tsp ground cinnamon

Blackcurrant (or blueberry) galette

My dad had a couple of blackcurrant bushes in the garden and though we never got as much fruit from them as we did from the raspberry canes, they were still a joy – a true taste of summer. And though Mum always made jam with the raspberries, it was jelly she made with the blackcurrants. I remember the drip-drip of the juice splashing from the ancient jelly bag into the bowl below, before being boiled up with sugar into beautiful translucent jelly, ready to be spread on Scotch pancakes for tea.

Because blackcurrants are so seasonal, the alternative is to make this with blueberries, which are readily available all year. And if you can find blaeberries (the Scottish word for bilberries) in the hills and mountains, these would be best.

For me, blaeberries are also reminiscent of my time spent as a student in the south of France working as an au pair. The Zelt family lived in Arles, in Provence, which was oppressively hot in the summer, so they headed to the Pyrenees for a week to take in the fresh mountain air. I remember the rickety old house we stayed in, perched on a cliff side in a tiny mountain village. Most days we would drive into the forests and woods to pick 'myrtilles', the native blueberries, which are not dissimilar in flavour, though far more intense since they are wild, to the farmed blueberries which we can nowadays buy so easily.

As we drove slowly along the mountain tracks, there would suddenly be a cry of 'Myrtilles!' from the back, as the children spotted the berries. Everyone then leapt out of the car and we began to gather as many of the sweet berries as possible. Once home, since there was no customised tart tin in the kitchen, Madame Zelt made 'tarte aux myrtilles' free-form, on a baking sheet.

During my year after university in the north of Finland, I enjoyed lots of free-form, open fruit pies and tarts. My Finnish friends also preferred to bake them on trays instead of within the confines of pie tins. There they used lingonberries or bilberries that they had foraged from the woods.

Serve this pie – which pedants may wish to call a 'galette' – in slices with some thick yoghurt. And if you want to smarten it up and forget the free-form style, then do exactly the same as the recipe, but tuck it all neatly into a 28cm tart tin.

Serves 6

•

For the pastry

250g plain flour

25g icing sugar

150g butter, diced

1 egg

•

For the filling

600g blackcurrants or blueberries

caster sugar: 125g for the blackcurrants; 75g for the blueberries + extra

1 rounded tbsp semolina

1 medium egg white, for glazing

For the pastry, place the flour in a food processor with the sugar and diced butter. Whizz until it resembles breadcrumbs, then, while the machine is running, add the egg and process briefly, until it just starts to clump together. You can do this by hand by rubbing the butter into the flour and sugar, then adding the egg to bind. Wrap in cling film and chill for half an hour or so.

Lightly butter a large baking sheet.

Roll out the pastry to a thin circle about 38–40cm in diameter. Don't worry about it being a perfect circle; remember this is a casual pie, not one that's likely to win prizes for 'Best in Patisserie'.

Tuck in the edges a little and cover with cling film, then chill again for another half hour or so.

For the filling, if you are using blackcurrants, wash and pat well dry, then remove them from their thin stems before mixing in a bowl with 125g of sugar and the semolina. For blueberries, just wash, pat dry and mix with 75g of sugar and the semolina.

Preheat the oven to 200°C.

Remove the baking sheet from the fridge. Pile the blackcurrants or blueberries into the centre and then fold in the edges: turn the pastry in, to form a wide crust all around. Most of the fruit will still be showing. You may need to patch up the sides with bits of pastry but do not worry if it all looks a little haphazard. This is the charm of this pie.

Using a pastry brush, brush all over the crust with some egg white, then sprinkle with a little caster sugar.

Bake for about 30 minutes or until the pastry is golden brown and the bubbling juices are oozing alluringly out. Wait for 20 minutes or so before cutting and serving.

Fly cemetery

One of my childhood treats was a fly cemetery. It was not part of my mum's baking repertoire, only ever bought at the local baker's. A moist, sticky filling of dried fruit (usually just currants, but I prefer a mixture with raisins too) is encased in a good short pastry – always with a welcome crunch from the sugar on top.

The filling in most recipes is simply dried fruit, sugar and softened butter, but instead of the butter I love using custard to bind it. I first saw this idea in *Dundee Kitchen*, written by the wonderful TV cook and fellow Dundonian Grace Mulligan. As she said, this is a good way to use up leftover custard.

Known simply as fruit slice in other parts of Britain, it is also popular in Northern Ireland. According to Northern Irish chef Paula McIntyre, they are called a Flies' Graveyard as well as Fly Cemetery. As she says, this is not the prettiest description . . . for something that is so incredibly tasty.

Place the flour, almonds, icing sugar and butter in a food processor and whizz until it resembles breadcrumbs. Then, with the machine running, add the egg and egg yolk and process briefly until it begins to clump together. Tip the mixture onto a piece of cling film and bring together with your hands into a ball, then flatten between the cling film layers. Chill for half an hour.

Butter a 23 × 23cm square tin.

Roll out the pastry to fit the base and a little way up the sides of your prepared tin. Roll out the remaining dough to fit the top. Wrap the top in the cling film (to prevent it drying out) and chill this and the base in the tin for an hour or so (or overnight).

When you are ready to bake, preheat the oven to 200°C.

For the filling, mix the dried fruit, sugar and spice together, then add the custard, stirring well to combine.

Tip the filling onto the base of the prepared tin, moisten the edges with water and top with the pastry lid. Press down a little, then use the tines of a fork around the edges to seal. Prick all over lightly with a fork.

Place in the oven for 15 minutes, then reduce the temperature to 180°C and continue to bake for another 15 minutes or until golden brown. Remove from the oven and sprinkle over some caster sugar, then allow to cool completely before cutting into squares.

Makes 24

•

For the pastry

300g plain flour

50g ground almonds

50g icing sugar

175g butter, diced

1 egg + 1 egg yolk

•

For the filling

250g raisins

150g currants

75g light muscovado sugar

1 tsp mixed spice

3 rounded tbsp thick custard

caster sugar, to sprinkle

8
Biscuits
& cookies

Chocolate-bottom coconut macaroons

Petticoat tails

Shortbread

Aga shortbread

Pitcaithly bannock

Bride's Bonn

Oaty jammy dodgers

Berry shortbread crumble squares

Tablet cookies

Empire (or Belgian or German) biscuits

Custard creams

Oaties

Anzac biscuits

Afghan biscuits

Green tea and choc chip cookies

Aztec cookies

Brookies

Dulse and nigella biscuits

Cheese and caraway biscuits

Introduction

Biscuits in my house were shop-bought. There were digestives, rich teas, bourbons, gypsy creams, custard creams, Abernethy . . . and of course foil-wrapped chocolate biscuits for special occasions: Club Orange, Penguins, KitKats. And chocolate digestives (with milk chocolate; who wants a dark chocolate digestive?) for not quite such special occasions, but we were still never allowed more than one at a sitting.

One exception to the 'shop-bought for biscuits' rule was shortbread. Everyone's mum baked shortbread. Some was crumbly, some meltingly tender, some delightfully gritty. I loved it all. Add a layer of caramel and a coating of chocolate, call it millionaires' shortbread, and I was in heaven.

The only other exception was empire biscuits, often baked at home and seen in those biscuit tins of old. My mum's had a glacé cherry on top. Other – luckier – children had jelly tots.

Cookies – massive American biscuits – came later and, boy, did we get into them in a big way. No wonder. There is little nicer than a warm chocolate chip cookie with a cup of tea or glass of cold milk.

Biscuits are part of my Scottish upbringing. When I stayed at my auntie Muriel's house in Dundee, mornings began with her bringing me a cup of tea in bed and a Royal Scot biscuit perched on the saucer. It was bliss!

Both biscuits and cookies are always welcome, home-baked, freshly made.

Previous page: Custard creams, p. 229
Below: Empire (or Belgian or German) biscuits, p. 227

Chocolate-bottom
coconut macaroons

————————

These are a real taste of my childhood. My mum made what she called macaroon tartlets, with a lovely mixture of desiccated coconut, sugar and eggs atop some raspberry jam in a little pastry case. I have taken the concept of the filling and made it into macaroons that you can then dip into molten chocolate. Or not, as you wish.

They are moist inside, slightly crunchy outside, and when dipped into chocolate, they remind me of an old television advert for Bounty, 'a taste of paradise' . . .

————————

Line two baking trays with parchment paper. Preheat the oven to 180°C.

Place the milk, coconut and egg whites in a bowl and combine well, then spoon into 20 little mounds – pile them high, do not spread them out – on the trays, spacing well apart.

Bake for about 15 – 18 minutes, swapping the trays around halfway through to ensure even cooking. They are ready when golden brown on top and firm to the touch.

Remove and leave on the baking parchment to cool.

Melt the chocolate (I use the microwave, for about 3 – 4 minutes, stirring halfway). One at a time, dip the bottom of each macaroon into the melted chocolate, letting it come up the sides a little too, then place these directly onto a clean piece of baking parchment on a board. Allow to cool until set – or pop in the fridge to hasten things along. I usually do this, as I just can't wait!

Makes 20

•

1 × tin (397g) condensed milk

250g desiccated coconut

3 egg whites

200g best quality chocolate
(I like half dark, half milk)

Petticoat tails

Makes 16 triangles

•

175g butter, softened

75g caster sugar + extra to sprinkle on top

175g plain flour

pinch of salt

75g fine semolina or rice flour (or cornflour)

Shortbread has been made over the centuries in finger-shaped biscuits, round biscuits and a full round 'cake' known as petticoat tails. The origin of the name of these dainty shortbread biscuits is interesting. Some believe it to be a corruption of the French *petites galettes*, which is taken to mean little cakes. Given the Auld Alliance and the culinary interchange between France and Scotland, this is a possibility.

Or perhaps it is even more simple. Is it, in fact, to do with the shape of the biscuits? The wedges are identical in shape to the individual gores of the full, bell-hooped petticoats worn by the ladies at court, probably at the time of Mary, Queen of Scots in the sixteenth century; she was said to be fond of them.

A trick to ensure perfectly even petticoat tails is not to roll out the dough to completely fill the tin but to allow it to be just a little shy of the edges. This mean the dough spreads out during baking to fill the tin and cooks evenly.

Classically, there would be a round circle in the middle of the triangles, but this is seldom seen nowadays.

I like to use fine semolina or rice flour, but if you prefer a more melting texture, use cornflour.

___

Butter two 17cm sandwich tins (or one 25cm tin). Preheat the oven to 150°C.

Cream the butter and sugar together until pale; this will take 4–5 minutes in a food mixer or longer by hand.

Now add the flour, a good pinch of salt and the semolina/rice flour (or cornflour), a tablespoonful at a time, only adding more when incorporated. When all mixed in, bring together with your hands and divide into one large or two medium balls.

Roll out each ball (either by pressing with your palms if you have cold hands or with a very light touch of a rolling pin, if your hands are hot) to a circle just a little shy of your prepared tins, then pop into the tin. Prick all over with a fork (ensure you go right through to the base) and 'scallop' the edges by nicking round the edges with the end of a spoon. If you have time, chill the tins for about 10 minutes, as the dough will be slightly warm, depending on how hot your hands tend to be.

Place in the oven for 35–40 minutes for the small tins, and 40–50 minutes for the large tin, until the biscuits are a pale golden brown. Remove the tins to a wire rack, cut each of the two small circles into eight triangles, and the large circle into 16, and sprinkle over some sugar. Leave for 15–20 minutes or so, then remove from the tin while still a little warm but firm enough to be removed. Leave on a wire rack until cold.

Shortbread

Makes 24 – 30

•

225g slightly salted butter, softened

100g caster sugar, plus extra for dredging

225g plain flour

100g cornflour, rice flour (ground rice) or semolina

There are so many different recipes for shortbread, from my granny's wartime recipe, with its lower than usual ratio of butter to flour, in keeping with rationing, to lavish ones with toffee, chocolate or warm spices like cardamom or ginger.

The main things about shortbread are the buttery taste and the texture, which can vary from crunchy to melting. If you use rice flour (ground rice) or semolina, it is nicely crunchy; using cornflour gives you a melt-in-the-mouth texture. You can, of course, make it using only flour, but I think it is more interesting by adding cornflour, semolina or rice flour.

Also, you can use half self-raising flour and half plain, for a nice, light texture. If you make it with gluten-free flour and rice flour, the shortbread will be even crunchier than usual.

In her book *The Scots Household*, written in the eighteenth century, Marion Lochhead describes tea parties where the hostess 'must have a plate of bun and one of shortbread – either in a cake, broken into bits, or in little, round nickety Tantallon cakes, or in the favourite "petticoat tails"'. (Tantallon cakes are rounds of shortbread biscuits flavoured with grated lemon zest.) Many years on, shortbread still appears at all the best parties, from Christmas to Hogmanay and throughout the year, as well as making welcome appearances on your saucer when you have a coffee or tea in a Scottish café.

This is the only recipe where I use slightly salted butter; if you only have unsalted, add a good pinch of salt.

Butter a swiss-roll tin (23 × 33cm). Preheat the oven to 150°C.

Place the butter in a food mixer and beat together with the sugar until pale: this will take up to 5 minutes. Alternatively beat by hand.

Add the flour and the cornflour/rice flour/semolina, processing only very briefly until just combined. Do not over process.

Tip into the prepared tin, then, using floured hands, press down to level the surface. Prick all over with a fork, then, if time permits, chill in the fridge for 10 – 15 minutes. Bake for 35 – 45 minutes or until a pale golden brown.

Remove from the oven, shake over some sugar from a dredger, then cut into squares or fingers. Leave to cool, then remove from the tin onto a wire rack.

Aga shortbread

There is a choice of ingredients in this recipe, which is based on Jo Sutherland's at the Carfraemill hotel in the Borders. You can use plain or self-raising flour, and also caster or icing sugar. Jo always used to bake it with icing sugar and self-raising flour, for a wonderfully melting texture. But if you make it with plain flour and caster sugar, you will have more of a delightfully welcome light crunch. Both are delicious and also easy.

Though it can be baked in a regular oven, it was Jill Pattle who gave me her Aga shortbread instructions, as her shortbread is legendary in Linlithgow, where her daughter Sally runs the brilliant bookshop Far from the Madding Crowd. She also runs the hugely successful Further From Book Festival, and when I am there, both Jill and Sally bake fabulous traybakes and cakes for the audience. Gingerbread, carrot cake, my mum's sultana cake and, my other favourite, Jill's Aga shortbread are just some of the treats for the crowds. The baking is so good I do wonder if the audience is there to listen to me ramble on about cookery or fiction, or to eat the delicious bakes. I think I know the answer . . .

Butter a swiss-roll tin (23 × 33cm) and, if using a regular oven, preheat it now to 150°C.

Place the butter and sugar in a mixer or food processor and cream until pale. Once well amalgamated, add the flour, a good pinch of salt and the cornflour a tablespoon at a time, and continue to blend briefly, until thoroughly combined. Tip into the buttered tin and, using floured hands, press down so it is level. Prick all over and now, if you have time, chill for 10 minutes or so.

In a regular oven, bake for 45 – 55 minutes.

In the Aga, pop the tin into the Roasting oven for 5 – 10 minutes only. Then remove and gently smooth the top with a palette knife, not really pressing down too much. Return it now to the Baking oven, for a further 30 – 40 minutes, until done. Check after 30 minutes: what you are looking for is a uniform pale golden colour all over. Do not allow it to become golden brown.

Remove and cut into squares or bars. Leave for at least 10 minutes before carefully decanting onto a wire rack to cool.

Makes 24 – 30

•

280g butter, softened

140g caster sugar
(or icing sugar)

280g plain flour
(or self-raising)

pinch of salt

140g cornflour

Pitcaithly bannock

I have adapted this recipe from one I found in a handwritten book I was privileged to look at in the National Library of Scotland, written by a Margaret Stewart in 1799. She lived in the manse in Erskine, near Glasgow, where her husband was the minister.

The addition of caraway seeds, nuts and peel was commonplace in those days. For us, it is so easy to buy almonds already blanched, but we tend to forget that before starting to make this in the olden days the cook would have had to blanch the almonds before chopping.

Before baking, the Pitcaithly bannock was often decorated. F. Marian McNeill writes in her recipe: 'Ornament, if desired, with large caraways and orange peel.'

The Pitcaithly bannock was a festive shortbread, baked for special occasions, and was traditionally baked in a round, rather like a round of petticoat tails, and so you can also make my recipe here in two small sandwich tins, 18cm each, following the final instructions for Petticoat tails (p. 216).

***

Makes about 24

•

225g butter, slightly softened

100g caster sugar + extra

200g plain flour

100g rice flour (ground rice)

1 rounded tsp caraway seeds

40g almonds, finely chopped

grated zest of 1 small orange

pinch of salt

***

Lightly butter a swiss-roll tin (23 × 33cm). Preheat the oven to 150°C.

Place the butter in a food mixer with the sugar. Cream until pale: this will take at least 3 – 5 minutes or double that time if beaten by hand. Add the flour and rice flour, and the flavourings, with a pinch of salt, and process very briefly – until just brought together. Do not over process.

Tip into the tin and, using floured hands, press down all over to level the surface. Prick all over with a fork, then bake for 40 – 45 minutes, or until uniformly pale golden brown.

Shake over some sugar from a dredger, then cut into squares or fingers. Leave for 5 – 10 minutes, then carefully remove to a wire rack to cool completely.

Bride's Bonn

Makes 2 rounds
(cut into 8 triangles each)

•

200g butter, softened

100g caster sugar

200g self-raising flour

pinch of salt

100g medium oatmeal

Bride's Bonn is a traditional Shetland bake – formerly, it was a sweet oat bannock, then later it became a thick round of shortbread. This was broken over a bride's head by the women as she entered the house for the wedding party after the church service. The concept was rather like confetti in our days. Though with the shortbread, guests would scrabble for pieces to take home and put under their pillows, as they were meant to have special attributes that enhanced dreams. Bride's Bonn was also traditionally known as dreaming bread.

I have introduced self-raising flour to the regular oatmeal shortbread, as it makes it lighter and more short in texture. The oatmeal, being heavier, makes it too dense.

This is one of my favourite shortbreads: light, nutty and moreish.

Lightly butter two 18cm sandwich tins. Preheat the oven to 150°C.

Cream the butter and sugar together until pale. This will take 4–5 minutes in a food mixer. You will need a little longer by hand.

Now add the flour and the oatmeal, a tablespoonful at a time, only adding more when incorporated, along with a pinch of salt. When all are mixed in, bring together with your hands and tip into the prepared tins. Using floured hands, press down, with the palms of your hands, so the mixture levels out.

Prick all over with a fork (ensure you go right through to the base) and 'scallop' the edges by nicking round them with the end of a spoon or the tines of a fork.

Place in the oven for 35–40 minutes until golden brown. Remove the tins to a wire rack, cut each into eight triangles, then leave for 15 –20 minutes. Remove from the tin while still a little warm but firm enough to be removed. Leave on the wire rack until cold.

Oaty jammy dodgers

Not quite jammy dodgers, which are two biscuits sandwiched together with jam, and not quite thumbprint cookies, a shortbread-like biscuit with a blob of jam in a dent. These are crunchy oaty biscuits that are enhanced with a dollop of jam and are extremely popular with grown-ups and children alike.

Line two baking sheets with parchment paper. Preheat the oven to 180°C.

Cream the butter and sugar well together, then add the egg with a spoonful or so of the weighed flour. Beat well together, then add the remaining flour, a pinch of salt and the bicarbonate of soda. Fold in the oats, combining well.

Using two dessertspoons, place little balls of the mixture onto the baking sheets. Dip your thumb into a little flour and make a shallow thumbprint in the centre of each, then fill each with a small spoonful of jam. (You will need about half a teaspoon in each.)

Place in the oven and bake for about 12 – 15 minutes, swapping the trays halfway, until the biscuits are golden brown and just firm to the touch.

Leave on the trays for about 5 minutes, then remove them to a wire rack to cool completely.

Makes 12 – 14

•

110g butter, softened

75g light muscovado sugar

1 medium egg, lightly beaten

75g plain flour

pinch of salt

½ teaspoon bicarbonate of soda

110g porridge oats

raspberry or strawberry jam

Berry shortbread crumble squares

Makes 16–20

•

For the filling

500g frozen berries

125g caster sugar

1 rounded tbsp cornflour

1 tbsp cold water

•

For the shortbread

250g plain flour

100g caster sugar

225g block of Stork margarine
(or butter), chilled and diced

50g porridge oats

This recipe is based on the wonderful Isle of Luing home bakers' vegan shortbread squares. Mary Braithwaite – one of the island's talented bakers – also makes the most fabulous sourdough bread in her tiny artisan bakery in Cullipool, the main village on the island. The other village on Luing has the splendid name of Toberonochy.

Mary uses block Stork to make this recipe vegan, and it is indeed a delicious bake, but it can also be made with the same amount of butter instead of the Stork for a non-vegan version. She uses a pack of frozen mixed summer fruits, but I always look out for the packs without strawberries, as they tend to go rather mushy. My favourite contains raspberries, brambles, and red and black currants. The leftover berry mixture is delicious stirred into yoghurt for breakfast or dolloped onto porridge.

The resulting shortbread squares are delicious, served with a cup of tea, at any time of day.

First prepare the filling. Tip the berries (straight from the freezer) into a pan and heat until they begin to defrost and their juices run. Add the sugar and stir to combine, continuing to heat gently until the sugar dissolves and the berries begin to soften. Increase the heat and bring to the boil, stirring.

Mix the cornflour with a tablespoon of cold water into a paste and add this slowly to the pan, stirring constantly, then continue to cook until thickened. This should only take a few minutes. Remove from the heat and tip into a bowl. Leave to cool.

Butter and line a 23cm square baking tin (about 5cm depth). Preheat the oven to 180°C.

Place the flour, sugar and margarine/butter into a food processor and pulse briefly until it looks a little clumpy. Tip about three-quarters of this mixture into the tin and press down to create a firm, even base.

Spoon about four rounded tablespoons of the cooled berry mixture over the base, leaving a margin all around the edges. This is about two-thirds of the mixture; save the rest for breakfast.

Add the oats to the remaining shortbread mixture, pulse briefly, then sprinkle this evenly over the fruit. Press down lightly.

Bake for 40–45 minutes or until golden brown. Cool completely before cutting and removing from the tin.

Tablet cookies

Makes 20

•

125g butter, softened

75g light muscovado sugar

1 egg

150g plain flour

½ tsp bicarbonate of soda

125g tablet, cut into chunks

The scene is a large garden somewhere in Scotland on a warm, summer afternoon. The occasion is the church garden fête. And even though the date is circa 1965, I still remember so vividly queuing up (probably in my best cotton frock) at the cake and candy stall before the fête had even been opened, with my 3d to buy a bar of tablet. And I was not alone. Tablet, neatly wrapped in waxed paper, was first to sell out at any fête, sale of work or bazaar, and the people in the queue stretching past the bric-a-brac and tombola stalls invariably ignored the lady in the big hat who was officially opening the fête, while attempting (politely – it was a church fête, remember) to edge up the queue a little more.

Almost unknown south of the border, tablet is one of Scotland's oldest types of confectionery. There is reference to it in Marion Lochhead's *The Scots Household in the Eighteenth Century*. She writes, 'Barley-sugar, tablet, crokain [from the French *croquant*, meaning crunchy] are all old and honourable Scots confections.'

By 1929, when F. Marian McNeill wrote *The Scots Kitchen*, milk had been added to the original recipe, which used water and sugar, for her recipe entitled 'Scots tablet' which now includes granulated sugar, thin cream or milk, and flavouring. For the latter, she suggests cinnamon, coconut, fig, ginger, lemon, orange, pepper-mint, walnut or vanilla.

Having been brought up on tablet embellished with nothing other than its neatly packaged waxy wrapping, I like it only with the merest hint of vanilla, pure and simple. If ever there was a childhood memory to evoke happy thoughts of sunshine, laughter and lush green gardens, it is an indulgent bite of tablet.

———————

Cream the butter and sugar together (I do this in my food processor, but you can do by hand). Add the egg and mix again, then add the flour and bicarbonate of soda. Once it is all well blended, add the tablet and blitz briefly using the pulse button (or stirring together by hand).

Spoon the softish mixture onto a large sheet of cling film and roll into a log. Either chill well for a couple of hours, or even better, pop in the freezer for half an hour.

Line two baking sheets with parchment paper. Preheat the oven to 180°C.

Once the dough is hard, cut into 20 cookies with a sharp or serrated knife and place, slightly apart, on the baking sheets. Bake for 10–12 minutes, swapping the trays around halfway through. They'll be slightly soft but will firm up a little on cooling.

Leave on the tray for a couple of minutes, then carefully remove to a wire rack to cool.

Empire (or Belgian or German) biscuits

These biscuits have always been hugely popular in Scotland. In my house they were called Belgian biscuits, but before the First World War they were known as German biscuits and sometimes still are. Nowadays they are most commonly known as Empire biscuits. Basically a sandwich of two shortbread-like biscuits, with jam in the middle and glacé icing with a cherry on top, they are a very strong link back to my childhood.

Some more modern recipes have a jelly baby or a jelly tot on top, instead of the cherry, and I must admit this is far more welcome to my grandchildren.

My recipe is based on one in an old SWRI cookbook, which uses a little raising agent, though nowadays most bakers leave this out. Their recipe also adds an egg, which I do too, to help bind the mixture. They sandwich the biscuits together with jelly, not jam. I mix some cornflour in with the flour to add to the melting texture and the result is a lovely short, light biscuit that is all too easy to eat. The word moreish was invented for these biscuits.

Line two or three baking sheets with parchment paper. Preheat the oven to 180°C.

First, place the butter and sugar in a food mixer (or beat by hand), then cream together until light and fluffy.

Mix together the flours and baking powder. Add the egg to the butter mixture and a couple of spoonfuls of the flour mixture and combine again, then gradually add all the flour, combining until the dough leaves the sides of the bowl clean.

Remove with your hands and place on a lightly floured board. Using a rolling pin, roll out to a thickness of 1cm (no more), then, using a fluted cutter, cut out into rounds. I like to use a 6cm cutter, but you can use smaller or bigger.

Place these on the baking sheets and bake for 12 – 15 minutes, or until a light golden colour. Swap the sheets round from top to bottom if you have more than one sheet in the same oven.

Remove to a wire rack to cool.

Make the icing by placing the icing sugar in a bowl and adding just enough cold water to form a thick but spreadable icing.

Once the biscuits are cold, sandwich them together with some jam, then, using two teaspoons, top with a circle of icing, then finally add a glacé cherry or jelly tot.

Makes 16 – 20

•

200g butter, softened

100g caster sugar

250g plain flour

100g cornflour

¼ tsp baking powder

1 medium egg

•

For the middle, icing and top

200g icing sugar, sifted

2 – 3 tbsp water

jam or jelly (whichever flavour you like; raspberry jam is traditional)

a few glacé cherries, halved (or jelly babies or tots)

Custard creams

Some biscuits are not dissimilar to their commercially produced namesakes. A home-baked digestive biscuit more or less tastes the same, as does good quality commercial shortbread (which means, made with butter only). But a custard cream? Never. Different shape, different texture, different filling.

The only similarity between a packet of custard creams and a home-baked version is the colour. Home-baked custard creams are light and melting and filled with a thick buttercream. They are divine and need nothing else but a cup of tea – and willpower to not eat too many, they are so moreish. To my knowledge this has never been an adjective ascribable to a supermarket packet of custard creams.

This recipe is based on Petra Archibald's. Her family run the brilliant Oyster Shed on the eastern side of Loch Gruinart on Islay. I first visited the oyster farm almost two decades ago to see the oysters, farmed as a sideline to cattle, sheep, barley and oats. They now have a hugely popular café / restaurant in the most stunning of locations above the loch, and as you sit eating one of Petra's home-bakes, you can see shoveler ducks, barnacle geese, lapwing, dunlins . . . the list is endless. There are also seals basking on the shore or heading out to the northern end of the loch, where they surf along the breakwater. This idyllic Islay scene is enhanced by a delicious custard cream from Petra at the Oyster Shed.

Makes 8

•

170g butter, softened

55g icing sugar, sifted

170g self-raising flour

55g custard powder

•

For the filling

50g butter, softened

100g icing sugar, sifted

a few drops of vanilla extract

Line two baking trays with parchment paper. Preheat the oven to 180°C.

Cream the butter and icing sugar together till fluffy (I do this in my food mixer.), then gradually add the flour and custard till you have a smooth dough.

Divide into small balls – about 16 – rolling them between your hands. Place them, well spaced apart, on two baking trays. Using a fork dipped into flour (I just dip mine directly into the flour bag), press down gently to leave the characteristic lines, and also to flatten them slightly.

Bake for about 12 – 15 minutes, swapping the trays around halfway through.

Remove to a wire rack to cool while you make the icing. Beat the butter until soft, then gradually add the icing sugar with a few drops of vanilla. Once cool, sandwich the biscuits together with a spoonful of the buttercream.

Oaties

Makes 12 – 15

·

150g butter, softened

50g caster sugar

75g light muscovado sugar

125g porridge oats

75g self-raising flour

½ tsp bicarbonate of soda

pinch of salt

These easy biscuits are crunchy, light and buttery, ideal to go with morning coffee or an afternoon cup of tea.

For a change, you can add a handful of raisins to make that all-American favourite, oatmeal raisin cookies.

Line two baking sheets with parchment paper. Preheat the oven to 180°C.

Cream the butter and sugars together until smooth, then add the oats, sift in the flour and bicarbonate of soda, and add the pinch of salt. Stir until thoroughly combined, then, using floured hands, roll into balls and place well apart (they will spread) on the baking sheets.

Place in the oven for about 15 minutes, swapping over the baking sheets halfway through, until golden brown. Leave for a couple of minutes, then remove to a wire rack to continue cooling.

Anzac biscuits

These are traditionally eaten on Anzac Day (25 April) in Australia and New Zealand. Anzac stands for Australian and New Zealand Army Corps: they are a tribute to the forces who fought in the invasion of the Gallipoli peninsula in 1915.

Buttery and crisp, they also have a lovely crunch from the coconut and oats.

Line two large or three medium baking trays with parchment paper. Preheat the oven to 160°C.

Melt the butter, syrup and sugar together (I do this in a microwave; you can also do so in a saucepan). Once melted, tip in the remaining ingredients with a pinch of salt.

Combine well, then place small spoonfuls (using 2 dessertspoons) onto the prepared baking trays. Space them well apart, as they spread while cooking.

Bake for 12 – 15 minutes until golden brown.

Remove and leave on their trays for 5 – 10 minutes, then remove to a wire rack to cool.

Makes 24 – 30

•

150g butter

1 rounded tbsp golden syrup

75g caster sugar

100g plain flour

100g porridge oats

1 tsp bicarbonate of soda

50g desiccated coconut

pinch of salt

Afghan biscuits

Makes 12 – 14

•

200g butter, softened

100g caster sugar

150g plain flour

40g cocoa powder

100g cornflakes

•

For the topping

200g icing sugar

1 rounded tbsp cocoa powder

3 tbsp (approx.) hot water

12 – 14 walnut halves

Usually just called Afghans, I discovered these crunchy, chocolately biscuits on my first trip to New Zealand and I was hooked. These and Hokey Pokey ice cream are two of the things I simply have to have when I'm lucky enough to visit. As well as the fabulous seafood, obviously.

My daughter-in-law, Katie, was brought up in New Zealand and my recipe is based on hers. It is incredibly easy.

There are various theories about the origin of the biscuit's name, but my favourites are that it comes from either their similarity to the rugged landscape of Afghanistan or its resemblance to the traditional Afghan hat, the pakol.

Line a large baking sheet with parchment paper. Preheat the oven to 180°C.

For the biscuits, cream the butter and sugar together well. I use a food mixer, but you can do it by hand. Mix together the flour and cocoa and add to the butter. Once combined, add the cornflakes and mix briefly.

Roll the mixture into 12 – 14 balls between your palms, place on the baking sheet (leaving a little room for spreading) and flatten each a little with a fork.

Bake for 15 – 20 minutes or until set. Leave for 10 minutes or so on the tin, then remove to a wire rack to cool.

Meanwhile, make the icing. Sift the icing sugar and cocoa together, then gradually add enough hot water to combine to a thick consistency: it should be spreadable, but not runny, or too thick.

Top each biscuit with some icing, then a walnut, and leave to set completely.

Green tea and choc chip cookies

I first tried matcha – finely ground powder of green tea leaves – in Japan, where I was on a press trip to visit a soy sauce factory. Everywhere we went we were offered tea, and on one occasion we experienced a full tea ceremony, made from ceremonial-grade matcha.

Used in cooking, the culinary grade of matcha is cheaper but also slightly less vibrant green, as the ceremonial variety is made from the youngest tea leaves which have the highest concentration of chlorophyll.

These cookies have a tinge of green and the grassy, slightly bitter flavour of the matcha is balanced perfectly by the sweetness of the chocolate. White chocolate is also good with matcha, as it is even sweeter, so, if you prefer, substitute white for milk here.

If you want a brighter green colour, use a little bit more matcha (a rounded tablespoon) or use ceremonial grade matcha instead.

Line two baking trays with parchment paper. Preheat the oven to 190°C.

Beat together the butter and sugar until creamy. I do this in my food mixer but you can do so by hand.

Mix together the flour, bicarbonate of soda and matcha, with a pinch of salt.

Add the egg to the creamed mixture with a spoonful of the flour mixture, then gradually add the remaining flour.

Once it is all combined, stir in the chocolate by hand.

Place dessertspoonfuls onto the lined baking sheets and bake for 11 – 12 minutes until pale golden and still slightly soft in the centre. If using two trays in one oven, swap around halfway through (and you might need a minute or two longer).

Leave on their trays for a minute or so, then remove with a spatula to a wire rack to cool.

Makes 16

•

125g butter, softened

125g caster sugar

150g plain flour

½ tsp bicarbonate of soda

1 tbsp green tea powder/matcha

pinch of salt

1 egg, beaten

150g best quality milk chocolate chips

233

Aztec cookies

Makes 22 – 24

•

175g walnuts,
roughly chopped

250g desiccated coconut

100g dried apricots,
roughly chopped

125g best quality dark/milk
chocolate (I like a mixture),
roughly chopped

1 × tin (397g)
condensed milk

This recipe is based on one from two American chefs, Mary Sue Milliken and Susan Feniger. Some years ago, I was lucky enough to eat at their fabulous restaurant, Bordergrill in Santa Monica, California, which used to serve fabulous Mexican food.

This recipe is a variation of theirs for *pajas*, which they say are reminiscent of the sticky coconut treats found in some Mexican sweet shops. They are incredibly easy to make. Even easier to eat.

Don't chop the chocolate, nuts or apricot too finely – you want good sized chunks for these.

———

Line two baking sheets with parchment paper. Preheat the oven to 160°C.

Mix the first four ingredients in a bowl and slowly pour in the condensed milk. Stir everything together thoroughly, then, once well mixed, drop 22 – 24 blobs, using two spoons (they are sticky), onto the baking sheets. I like to keep them as towering mounds, but gently flatten the tops a little if you prefer a flatter cookie shape.

Bake for 18 – 20 minutes or until golden brown. Allow to cool (to set a little) for at least 10 minutes before transferring to a wire rack to cool.

Brookies

Makes 20

•

350g best quality
dark chocolate

50g butter

225g caster sugar

3 eggs

1 tsp vanilla extract

80g cornflour

1 tsp baking powder

100g dark chocolate chips

a sprinkle of sea salt flakes
(Emma uses Islay's excellent
Orsay Sea Salt)

Gluten-free, these are a combination of brownie and cookie. They should have a crisp cracked shell and a soft centre. The recipe comes from Islay-based Emma Goudie, who runs a wonderful chocolate company, Islay Cocoa, where she uses many local ingredients, including Jura artisan sourdough bread and Orsay Sea Salt. Once made, the dough can be kept in the fridge for a few days, so you don't need to bake them all at once.

Break up the chocolate into a bowl and add the butter. Microwave or melt over a pan of simmering water until the chocolate and butter have melted together.

In a food mixer or with a hand mixer, beat the sugar, eggs and vanilla together until light and frothy.

With the mixer running, slowly pour in the chocolate mixture until combined. Add the cornflour and baking powder, and mix briefly until just combined.

Cover the bowl with cling film and refrigerate for at least 1 hour.

Line two large baking sheets with parchment paper. Preheat the oven to 180°C.

Using an ice-cream scoop or a tablespoon, form the dough into balls. Place on the baking sheets, spacing apart, then press lightly on the top, pressing in a few chocolate chips. Sprinkle with a little sea salt.

Bake for 13–15 mins.

Remove from the oven and cool slightly before removing them to a wire rack. They will become less fragile when cool.

Dulse and nigella biscuits

This wonderful recipe is from cook and food writer Fiona Bird, who lives on South Uist with her husband, Stephen, the local GP. Ever since she moved there, she has foraged for seaweed, which she then uses in the kitchen. Her recipes include fresh dulse, kelp, sea spaghetti, carragheen and sloke (called laver in Wales, and nori in Japan).

Fiona says it's important to take only as much as you need for a recipe; she snips off the seaweed with scissors, leaving the rest to continue growing. She also recommends rinsing the seaweed in situ, then rinsing again in several changes of fresh water once home.

This recipe makes delicious little savoury biscuits that are excellent served with a chilled glass of pre-dinner wine.

Makes 25

•

50g fresh dulse, roughly chopped

75g cold butter, diced

pinch of salt

125g plain flour

handful of nigella seeds (optional)

1 rounded tsp parmesan, finely grated

In a food processor, chop the rinsed seaweed as finely as possible. Add the butter, a pinch of salt and the flour. Using the pulse button, mix these ingredients together until almost blended.

Remove the dough from the food processor and knead briefly. Divide the biscuit dough in half and on a lightly floured surface roll two logs about 15cm in length.

Sprinkle the nigella seeds onto a sheet of greaseproof paper and roll each log back and forth to coat with seeds.

Trim the ends of the logs and wrap each in cling film. Refrigerate for 30 minutes.

Line two baking sheets with parchment paper. Preheat the oven to 190°C.

Remove the cling film and cut the dough into 2cm slices. Place the biscuits on the baking sheet and sprinkle sparingly with a little parmesan.

Bake for 15 minutes or until the biscuits are lightly golden. Leave to cool (and firm) on the baking tray.

Store in an airtight tin once cold.

Cheese and caraway biscuits

Makes 20

•

100g plain flour

1 tsp caraway seeds

100g parmesan, grated

100g butter, softened

Caraway adds an unusual flavour to these crispy savoury biscuits. Caraway was used often in centuries past in Scotland, mainly in cakes and shortbread. F. Marian McNeill has optional caraway seeds in her petticoat tails (which she says was a Meg Dods recipe). She also advocates them as an optional extra in Abernethy biscuits.

English seed cake always contained caraway seeds; there is reference to their inclusion by seventeenth-century herbalist John Parkinson, who wrote that caraway added relish to breads and cakes. They were also made into 'comfits' – caraway seeds coated in sugar and served as an aid to digestion.

There is a wonderful old Scottish recipe for seed cake in Mrs MacIver's *Cookery and Pastry* from 1773, reprinted in a limited edition by the library of Innerpeffray. In her book, the Edinburgh cookery teacher adds caraway seeds to her seed cake, along with ginger and cinnamon. She also gives a recipe for a 'common biscuit' which has eggs and sugar mixed together with flour and caraway seeds, then the mixture is dropped in spoonfuls onto paper, glazed with sugar, then baked.

Lady Clark of Tillypronie (whose recipes were written in the second half of the nineteenth century) has two recipes for caraway biscuits, both of which are sweet, one baked in a 'quick oven', the other in a 'slow oven'.

And it is not only the spice that is a link to the past; perhaps surprisingly, the use of parmesan is not new. Lady Clark has a recipe for macaroni and parmesan fritters; and for parmesan biscuits, which are not dissimilar to the following recipe, but with a little cayenne instead of caraway.

Serve these with drinks. They are particularly good with champagne!

Place the first three ingredients in a food processor, then add the butter in knobs. Whizz until combined, then, having removed the blade, bring the dough together with your hands.

Tip onto a large sheet of cling film and roll into a log shape, about 20cm long. Wrap tightly in the cling film, then chill for an hour or so.

Line two baking sheets with parchment paper. Preheat the oven to 180°C.

Cut into 20 slices and place on the baking sheets. They spread a little, so don't put them too close. Bake for 15 minutes or until golden. Leave for 10 minute or so, then remove to a wire rack to cool.

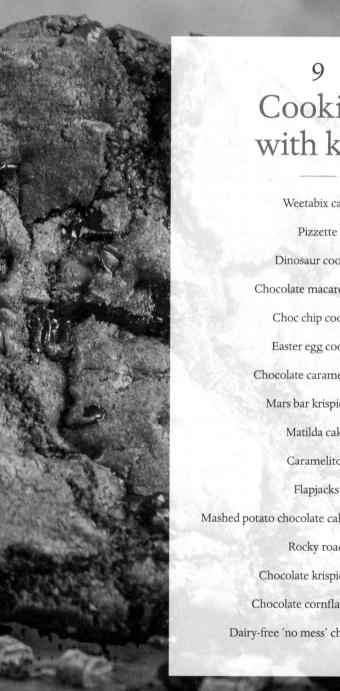

9
Cooking with kids

———

Introduction

One of the greatest pleasures of being a granny for me is cooking with the children. It takes me back to when I used to cook with my own three, and there are so many similarities – the mess, the spills, the bickering – but it boils down to the same thing: it's a joy to create something from scratch with children.

Hopefully, it also furnishes them with memories and gives them a basic grounding in the skills required to cook. During lockdown, when we were finally allowed to have the children in our house, we made bread, focaccia, pizza and, of course, scones, cakes, traybakes and cookies.

I was privileged to judge the *Bake Off* competition at the school where my friend Isabelle was a teacher. Seeing the concentration and enthusiasm on the faces of the pupils when confronted with the challenge of reading a recipe, measuring the ingredients, then mixing everything together to make delicious bakes was both humbling and inspirational.

Baking is something children love to do and, whatever the age, they can all take part. I've not given guidance about who is able to do what in this chapter – that's up to you as parent, carer or grandparent – but I can say that all the recipes in this chapter have been road-tested by a five-year-old and a three-year-old, some also with a couple of almost two-year-olds . . . with pretty high levels of success.

I'm not going to dictate what's best for adults to handle (sharp knives, etc.), what's best for children; common sense is required here as with all child care. So go get out the mixing bowls and the aprons: the fun is about to begin.

Previous page: Choc chip cookies, p. 249
Below: Making pizzette, p. 244

Weetabix cake

I found a recipe in a charity cookbook from the 1980s for a Weetabix cake and, since there is always Weetabix in my house (my third grandchild, Oliver, is a great fan), I had to give it a try.

After a few changes, and with the help of my chief tasters (the grand-children), the result is a wonderfully moist, well-textured fruit loaf that can be eaten as it is or spread with butter.

This latter is perhaps a Scottish peccadillo (we spread butter on digestive biscuits, gingerbread, Abernethy biscuits, cold cloutie dumpling and all sorts of (un-iced) fruit cake), but whether buttered or not, I recommend it.

This is one of the simplest recipes in this chapter to make with children: ingredients are combined in a bowl, then all tipped into a cake tin. Easy as that!

Butter a 1kg loaf tin and base-line with baking parchment.

Place the first three ingredients in a bowl and stir. Leave to soak for an hour or so.

Preheat the oven to 180°C.

Add the dried fruit and flour, stir to combine, then tip into the loaf tin.

Bake in the oven for about an hour, covering loosely with foil halfway through.

Leave till cool before turning out.

Makes 1 loaf

•

2 Weetabix

300ml whole milk

200g caster sugar

200g raisins/sultanas

225g self-raising flour

Pizzette

These are handy little pizzas for kids and canapés for grown-ups, but probably made more with kids in mind. They are also very easy for children to make.

Place the flour in a bowl with 2 teaspoons of salt. Stir in the yeast, then make a well in the centre.

Add the olive oil and about 350ml of tepid water – enough to make a softish dough. Turn onto a floured board and knead gently until smooth. It should take about 8 – 10 minutes.

Place in a bowl, cover and leave somewhere warm for an hour or so until risen, then punch down and place on a floured board. Roll out until fairly thin.

Lightly oil several baking sheets. Preheat the oven to 230°C.

Cut into about 40 small discs using a pastry cutter and place these on the baking sheets. Cover loosely and leave somewhere vaguely warm for half an hour or so, then concentrate on the toppings: spoon about a teaspoon of passata on each, then half a teaspoon of pesto, then some mozzarella.

If using any of the optional toppings, add these now. Season with salt and pepper, then bake in the preheated oven for about 10 minutes or until well risen.

Remove, then, using a teaspoon, drip one drop of olive oil over each pizzette before removing to a serving plate.

Serve warm.

Makes about 40

•

500g strong white flour

2 tsp salt

7g sachet fast-action
dried yeast

2 tbsp olive oil

350ml (approx.) tepid water

•

Toppings

175ml passata
(you'll need about a quarter
of a 700g bottle)

100g pesto sauce
(about half a jar)

150 – 200g mozzarella cheese,
grated or thinly sliced

freshly ground black pepper,
to season

olive oil

•

Optional toppings

black olives, pitted and sliced

salami, cut into pieces

mushrooms, chopped and
lightly sautéed

artichoke hearts, cooked
and chopped

Dinosaur cookies

These are a huge success with kids of all ages. I've done it with four-year-old Harris and almost two-year-old Iona, each batch with different results, but still as much fun.

Be sure to get good quality cutters, as little hands do tend to push them quite ruthlessly into the dough. If you can get the ones with protective handles, then these will be best for small, clumsy fingers.

To decorate, go mad with bright sprinkles and coloured icing.

Makes about 40
(number depends on size of
your cutters)

•

375g plain flour

150g icing sugar, sifted

250g butter, cut into small dice

1 egg yolk (you may also
need a drop or two of the
egg white)

•

To decorate

icing pens/sprinkles/
chocolate vermicelli/Smarties

Tip the first three ingredients into a food processor and whizz till thoroughly combined, then slowly add the egg yolk through the feeder tube, while the machine is running (adding a drop or two of egg white, if necessary, to bind). Stop the machine and bring the dough together with your hands, then shape into a flattish ball, wrap in cling film and chill for 20 minutes or so.

Line three large baking trays with parchment paper.

Roll out the dough on a floured board to a thickness of some 3mm (don't worry if it's slightly thicker, the cookies will just take a little longer to bake). Using the dinosaur cutters, cut out and place on the baking trays. It's perhaps worth mentioning that these cookies do not spread out while they bake, so you don't need to space them far apart. Chill for an hour or so.

Preheat the oven to 180°C.

Bake for 10–12 minutes (depending on thickness), swapping the trays around if you have more than one tray per oven. Remove to a wire rack to cool completely before icing in crazy dino patterns.

Chocolate macaroon bars

Macaroon bars seem to be a peculiarly Scottish sweet. Let's face it, who, apart from the Scots, with our renowned sweet tooth, would look at a leftover boiled potato and decide to mix it with sugar, then dip it in chocolate and coconut. For this is the old-fashioned – and undeniably the best – way of making these delicious bars, which used to rival tablet in popularly at church fairs and garden fêtes.

Nowadays commercial producers make them from sugar mixed with fondant and glucose.

This recipe came to me from the kitchen of Mary Coghill, from Brora in the north-east of Scotland. Now it is a treat and a joy for me to make them with the grandchildren, as they love both mashed potatoes and chocolate. What's not to like?

Makes 24–30

•

1 medium potato (preferably floury), peeled and boiled in unsalted water (boiled weight approx. 75g)

400–450g icing sugar

200–250g best quality chocolate (I like half milk, half dark)

125–150g desiccated coconut

Once boiled, drain the potato well and thoroughly dry. Place this very dry potato in a food mixer (not a food processor) and begin to mix with the flat beaters. Very gradually start adding the icing sugar (no need to use a sieve) a little at a time. Continue to add the sugar until the correct consistency is achieved: the paste should be smooth and stiff. (You can of course do this by hand, but it is arduous.)

Lightly butter a rectangular tin (approximately 23 × 18cm).

Tip in the mixture and smooth it out. Chill for an hour or so (or pop into the freezer for 20 minutes) until hard.

Meanwhile, melt the chocolate (in a shallow bowl, for easy dipping).

Toast the coconut by dry-frying, in batches, in a frying pan. Tip the coconut onto a large plate.

Now, cut the potato sugar mixture into bars and, working quickly, dip each bar into the chocolate (I use two forks), then dip into the coconut (again two forks). Place them on a sheet of baking parchment on a board to harden.

Choc chip cookies

This is based on one of the recipes from the school *Bake Off* competition that I judged for my friend Isabelle for many years. These cookies were so delicious, it really was almost impossible to pick the winners. But thankfully there were also prizes for Best Skills, Best Teamwork, Tidiest Work Station, etc., so, just like sports day these days, everyone was a winner. The children loved making them and it was a joy to taste each cookie.

I often make this dough in advance and freeze, to have freshly baked warm cookies: simply place the tablespoons of dough on a tray, spaced apart, and freeze uncovered till solid, then tip into a freezer bag. Bake from frozen.

Line two large baking sheets with parchment paper. Preheat the oven to 180°C.

Melt the butter. (I use the microwave.)

Place the flour in a bowl with the bicarbonate of soda and a quarter teaspoon of salt.

Place the sugars in a bowl, then add the melted butter and beat until combined.

Add the egg and yolk and stir well together, then add the flour mixture. Combine gently, then stir in the chocolate chips/chunks.

Place 6–8 tablespoons of the cookie dough on the baking sheets, spacing very well apart, and bake for 10–12 minutes, then remove carefully to a wire rack to cool.

Makes 6–8 large cookies

•

175g butter

250g plain flour

½ tsp bicarbonate of soda

¼ tsp salt

175g soft dark brown sugar

100g caster sugar

1 egg

1 egg yolk

300g best quality chocolate chips or chunks (milk/plain)

Easter egg cookies

Makes 24

·

175g butter

100g light brown sugar

½ tin condensed milk
(full tin weighs 397g)

1 tsp vanilla essence or paste

100g plain flour

200g self-raising flour

100g best quality milk
chocolate chunks

24 mini eggs
(one small packet)

This recipe is for a cookie that is almost chewy inside and with a lightly crisp outside. The addition of the condensed milk makes for a delightfully soft texture and it means you use a little less sugar than a regular cookie.

These are round cookies that spread a little as they bake, so ensure you space them well out on their baking trays. If you want to make crispier Easter egg cookies that are cut out with egg or bunny cookie cutters, use the Dinosaur cookie recipe on page 246, as these do not spread and will keep their Easter-themed shapes.

Line two large (or three medium) baking trays with parchment paper. Preheat the oven to 180°C.

Melt the butter until just molten, then cool a little before tipping it into a food mixer. (You can also do everything by hand by mixing the ingredients together in the order given.) Add the sugar and beat together, then add the condensed milk and vanilla and beat thoroughly until well mixed.

Add the flours gradually, beating until all are added, then finally add the chocolate chunks, mixing briefly to combine.

Using two dessertspoons, place balls of the dough onto the prepared baking trays, spacing well apart. Flatten slightly with your fingers, then bake for 10–12 minutes or until set and tinged with golden. Swap the trays around halfway.

Remove the trays and immediately press a mini egg into the top of each one, while the cookies are still warm.

Transfer to wire racks after a few minutes, then allow to become completely cold.

Chocolate caramel wafers

When you fly to the Scottish islands these days there is not only the heady anticipation of arriving on our beautiful isles, with their white sandy beaches and flower-studded machair. There is also the joy of eating a Tunnock's caramel wafer as you sip your inflight cup of tea. Loganair have given these out as snacks for some time now and they are not only welcome, they have become iconic, the red and gold wrappers always associated with Scotland.

I have been lucky enough to visit Tunnock's to see the famous caramel wafers being made. The smell was almost too much to bear, as I watched large sheets of wafer sandwiched together with caramel, cut into fingers then dunked in glossy chocolate. I was surprised to learn that the caramel wafer was only 'invented' in 1952; to me and most fellow Scots they had been with us forever. Tunnock's also make the exquisite snowballs that were served in the Italian ice-cream shops squashed between two wafers with scoops of milky ice cream in between. These were, perhaps unsurprisingly, called a Squasher.

This recipe bears a vague resemblance to Tunnock's wafers, though Tunnock's have five wafers and four caramel layers; mine have three wafer layers and two caramel.

Makes 15

•

15 (original) Ryvita crispbread

400g best quality milk chocolate

½ tin Nestlé caramel (full tin weighs 397g)

Spread a thick layer of the caramel onto a crispbread, top with another, then spread more caramel over that. Finish with a third crispbread. Continue until all 15 crispbreads are used up.

Melt the chocolate in a shallow bowl for easy dipping.

Using a very sharp knife, cut into three (with a gentle sawing motion, rather than a sudden tap). Using two forks, dip these in the chocolate, covering completely, then lay them out on greaseproof paper on a board to set.

Once the chocolate is hard, devour with a cup of tea, shut your eyes and imagine you are flying to one of Scotland's beautiful islands.

Mars bar krispie slice

Makes 20–24

•

6 Mars bars
(regular size, not mini)

2 tbsp golden syrup

150g butter

3 mugs of Rice Krispies
(a regular mug measuring
300ml)

300g best quality chocolate
(I like a mixture of 200g milk,
100g dark)

Who doesn't love this old favourite that combines Mars bars and Rice Krispies with a nice layer of chocolate on top?

This is an easy one for children to make, with supervision required with the microwave – oh and, as I discovered, removing the Mars bar wrappers. This can be challenging . . . I recall the Mars bar game we used to play at kids' parties when I was young: you sit in a circle and throw a dice. Whoever is first to get a six, starts to put on the many items of clothing laid out in the middle of the circle (hat / scarf / coat and, essentially, gloves, or worst of all mittens!). On a plate in front of you is a Mars bar, in its wrapper, with a fork and knife. Your aim is to remove the wrapper, then start to cut it into slices and devour it. Unless you have played this, you have no idea how difficult and frustrating this game is!

———————

Line a swiss-roll tin (23 × 33cm) with baking parchment.

Chop the Mars bars into pieces and place in a bowl with the syrup and butter. Melt in a microwave, then stir to combine.

Add the Rice Krispies and stir well, then tip into the tin. Level the top with the back of a spoon.

Melt the chocolate, then pour over the base, smoothing the top. Chill well, then cut into pieces.

Matilda cake

Makes 12 – 16 pieces

•

150g butter

100g caster sugar

2 tbsp golden syrup

300g self-raising flour

150g best quality
choc chips (half milk,
half dark)

Inspiration for this came from another charity cookbook, published in 1991. When I looked at it recently and saw a recipe for 'Matilda Cake' I knew I had to make it, since my oldest grandchild is called Matilda.

The recipe in the book uses glacé cherries rather than chocolate, but since my girl loves chocolate (like her granny) I have made substitutions. I have also made it slightly less sweet.

The texture of this is less cake, more shortcake-like (though not shortbread). Utterly delicious! Well done, Matilda.

———————

Butter a swiss-roll tin (23 × 33cm). Preheat the oven to 180°C.

Mix the first three ingredients, then melt them (I use the microwave to do this – you'll need about 2 – 3 minutes, stirring once).

Cool for about 15 – 20 minutes, then add the flour, then the chocolate chips. Combine well, then tip into the prepared tin, smoothing out the top with the back of a spoon.

Bake for about 18 – 20 minutes or until golden.

Remove and cut into squares or bars while still warm, then leave until completely cold before removing from the tin.

Caramelitos

Depending on their ages, kids can do most things here (apart from putting the tin into and taking out of the oven, and using the food processor – though they do like to press On and Off switches).

Line a 23 × 33cm swiss-roll tin with baking parchment. Preheat the oven to 180°C.

Blitz the oats in a food processor for a few seconds only, just till roughly ground, then tip into a large bowl with the next three ingredients. Stir well, then gradually add the melted butter.

Tip two-thirds of this into a prepared tin and press down. Kids like doing this with a potato masher. Scatter over 250g of the chocolate chips, then dollop over spoonfuls of the caramel, using two spoons – one to measure the caramel, the other to scrape it off the spoon.

Spoon over the remaining oat mixture and press down to roughly cover – this time don't use a potato masher, as the caramel will seep. Gentle hands suffice here, as it's a little sticky.

Bake for 20–25 minutes until firm and pale golden, then leave to cool before melting the remaining 50g of chocolate and drizzling it all over the top. Chill well before cutting into squares.

Makes 24

•

250g porridge oats

200g plain flour

300g light muscovado sugar

1 tsp bicarbonate of soda

250g butter, melted

300g best quality milk/dark chocolate chips

300g (approx.) Nestlé caramel (full tin weighs 397g), or you could use dulce de leche

Flapjacks

This is a recipe that is so easy I have done it with toddlers as well as their big brothers and sisters. Older children can almost do everything themselves, with supervision.

It is also incredibly versatile. Instead of adding seeds or chopped apricots, add raisins or dried blueberries. Instead of all dessicated coconut, add a third of the weight in coconut flakes, for added crunch. You can also leave out the seeds and add in some chopped toasted hazelnuts.

The only thing I would not change is using porridge oats. I've tried with larger jumbo oats, but it doesn't work as well and tends to fall apart. These freeze well and are a great favourite of little ones – and adults, too, at picnics on the hills.

Butter a swiss-roll tin (23 × 33cm). Preheat the oven to 180°C.

Melt the first three ingredients together (I do this in the microwave), then stir in the oats, flour and a pinch of salt. Stir in the remaining ingredients and tip into the lightly buttered tin, spreading out to level the surface. Children like to flatten it out using a potato masher.

Place on a large baking tin (in case of spillage) and put on the middle shelf of the oven until golden brown but still slightly soft – about 18–20 minutes – then remove to a wire rack.

Cut into bars while still hot, but only remove from the tin once cold.

Makes 18–24

•

175g butter

3 tbsp golden syrup

150g light muscovado sugar

350g porridge oats

50g plain flour

pinch of salt

½ tsp bicarbonate of soda

50g raisins, dried blueberries or chopped dried apricots

50g desiccated coconut or toasted chopped almonds

25g sunflower seeds

25g pumpkin seeds

Mashed potato chocolate cake
with toffee icing

•

For the cake

225g butter, softened

275g caster sugar

250g self-raising flour

50g cocoa

½ tsp baking powder

2 eggs

200g mashed potato, cooled
(no butter/milk added; ensure
really well mashed, no lumps)

100ml (approx.) milk

•

For the icing

125g butter, diced

150g dark muscovado sugar

100ml evaporated milk

1 tsp vanilla extract

250g icing sugar, sifted

I know, this sounds crazy . . . but it works! The potato lends a pleasing moistness to the cake, and the icing is caramelly and moreish.

The idea for this came about when I baked a cake for my grandson Oliver's second birthday. He was always rather difficult to feed, one day loving something, the next refusing to even try it. At nursery he would devour fruit; at home would not even take one tiny blueberry. But the one constant in his food 'likes' was mashed potato; this he would eat by the bowlful. So I wondered how it would be if I mixed some into his birthday cake? The good news is, you cannot taste the potato at all, there's just a lovely dense texture and a delicious cake.

The icing has a wonderfully dark toffee flavour. Decorate with candles and sprinkles for a birthday, or just a crumbled chocolate flake.

Butter and base-line two 20cm sandwich tins. Preheat the oven to 180°C.

For the cake, place the butter and sugar in a large bowl and cream them together until light and fluffy. You can also do this in a food mixer.

Sift the flour, cocoa and baking powder together.

Add the first egg to the butter mixture with some of the flour mixture and a spoonful of potato. Repeat with the flour and potato with the second egg, once fully amalgamated.

Once all the potato is incorporated, add the remaining flour mixture gradually, beating together after each addition and adding in enough milk to achieve the intended texture of thick and soft, yet not stiff.

Once fully combined, tip into the two prepared tins, smoothing the surfaces.

Bake in the oven for 25 – 30 minutes (swapping the tins around halfway through if necessary) until a toothpick, inserted into the middle, comes out clean.

For the icing, place the butter and sugar in a pan and heat over a gentle heat until the butter is melted and the sugar is dissolved. Stir well, add the evaporated milk and increase the heat. Stirring constantly, let it come to the boil, then remove from the heat and add the vanilla extract. Stir again, then allow to cool.

Pour it into a food mixer and add the icing sugar. Beat until smooth, then use to sandwich the two cakes together and spread over the surface.

Enjoy not only a slice of this moist cake, but also the frustration of the others, as you ask them to guess what's in the cake . . .

Rocky road

This is not dissimilar to the tiffin recipe on page 97, but studded with nuggets of marshmallow instead of honeycomb. Try to find mini marshmallows; if you can't, then cut whole marshmallows, but this can be a rather sticky process – it's best to do it with a fork and sharp knife.

The biscuits should be bashed in a plastic bag, not a food processor, as you don't want all crumbs; you want lots of chunky pieces, too. Toddlers love bashing the biscuits with a rolling pin – just ensure, with constant supervision, they don't bash their own little hands.

You can add 100g of raisins to the mix – and at Christmas, add perhaps 100g of dried cranberries for a nice festive touch.

First, butter and base-line a 20cm square baking tin.

Melt the butter, chocolates and syrup together. Stir well to combine.

Add the marshmallows and broken biscuits, combining thoroughly but gently (to avoid the marshmallows melting and the biscuits becoming more crumb-like).

Tip into the prepared tin, press down to level and allow to cool. Then mark into squares before placing in the fridge to chill completely before removing the squares.

Makes 20

•

150g butter

200g best quality milk chocolate

200g best quality dark chocolate

4 tbsp golden syrup

200g mini marshmallows

250g rich tea biscuits, broken into pieces (not all crumbs)

Chocolate krispie cakes
and cornflake cakes

Makes 12 cakes

•

For the krispie cakes

50g butter

2 tbsp golden syrup

1 tbsp caster sugar

2 heaped tbsp cocoa, sifted

about 75g Rice Krispies

•

For the cornflake cakes

200g best quality milk
chocolate

about 125g cornflakes

1 tsp sunflower oil

I remember both chocolate krispie cakes and cornflake cakes from my childhood. The first – which my mum made – are sticky, with cocoa and syrup in the recipe, and are more usually made with Rice Krispies. The second, which are crunchy not sticky, are made with chocolate, which in those days was Scotbloc, not proper chocolate. Nowadays when I make these with my grandchildren, I make them with proper chocolate. Apart from the delicious final taste, it means licking the bowl is a joy!

The quantities for the cornflake cakes are based on my Dundonian friend Vivienne's recipe, which she makes for her 12 grandchildren. They can be made into Easter 'nests' by inserting a mini egg into the centre while the mixture is still warm.

For either variety, start by setting 12 paper bun cases in a bun tray.

To make the krispie cakes, place the first four ingredients into a large microwaveable bowl, stir together and heat till everything is melted. Stir again, then add enough Rice Krispies to coat (you may not need them all). Using two spoons, one to scoop up the mixture, the other to push it into the case, fill the paper bun cases. Leave till cold before eating.

For the cornflake cakes, melt the chocolate (I do this in the microwave) and stir well. Mix in the oil and stir again. Tip enough of the cornflakes in to fully coat them, then spoon this mixture into the cases, pressing down a little – not too heavily, or you break up the flakes. Chill before serving.

Dairy-free 'no mess' chocolate cake

This is great fun to make – and unlike so many baking recipes where you need many different bowls and dishes, you need only your baking tin for this one, as you both mix and bake in the tin.

Children love making these, and I can attest that little ones as young as two can make the whole thing, obviously with supervision.

Oliver, my younger grandson, and I rustled these up in merely minutes for his older two siblings coming back from nursery and school. And it was only as he was sifting and mixing that I realised they are dairy-free: no eggs or milk or butter. Magic!

You can ice them with thick buttercream if you like, but they looks so gloriously shiny once baked I think they are good just as they are.

Grease a 20cm square cake tin with a little oil. Preheat the oven to 180°C.

Sift the flour and cocoa directly into the tin with a pinch of salt. Add the sugar and stir to combine everything.

Once fully mixed, mark out three long grooves along the edges and middle of the tin. Pour the oil along one groove, the vinegar into another and the vanilla into the third.

Now pour over the water and, using a wooden spoon, combine everything thoroughly, ensuring you get into all the corners to check there are no blobs of unmixed flour. If you have a small helper, try to do this subtly; they tend not to like their work criticised.

Place the tin in the oven for 18–20 minutes, or until a wooden cocktail stick comes out almost clean.

Remove from the oven, leave to cool for 10 minutes or so, then cut into squares. Remove to a plate once completely cool.

Makes 16

•

175g self-raising flour

2 rounded tbsp cocoa powder

pinch of salt

175g caster sugar

5 tbsp sunflower oil

1 tbsp white vinegar (I use white wine vinegar)

1 tsp vanilla extract

225ml cold water

Acknowledgements

Thanks to the following, for help with research and recipes.

Hilary Blackford
Cromlix House Hotel
Maggie Darling
Lara Haggerty
Tara Heron
Isabel Johnson
Paula McIntyre
Vivienne Miller
Sally Pattle
Isabelle Plews
Carol Tollerton

And thanks to Bethany Ferguson for her excellent food styling for Katie Pryde's wonderful photos.

Thank you also to Andrew Simmons and Deborah Warner at Birlinn for their professionalism and patience working on this book.

And a special mention to my wonderful agent Jenny Brown, for her hard work and enthusiasm: thank you.

Opposite: Fatty cutties, p. 77

Index of Recipes

Index